AF446879

# MEN WITH BLACK FACES

## The Tears of the Human Worms

by

Valentine J. Thomas & Albert J. Thomas II

DORRANCE PUBLISHING CO
EST. 1920
PITTSBURGH, PENNSYLVANIA 15238

The contents of this work, including, but not limited to, the accuracy of events, people, and places depicted; opinions expressed; permission to use previously published materials included; and any advice given or actions advocated are solely the responsibility of the author, who assumes all liability for said work and indemnifies the publisher against any claims stemming from publication of the work.

All Rights Reserved

Copyright © 2023 by Valentine J. Thomas & Albert J. Thomas II

No part of this book may be reproduced or transmitted, downloaded, distributed, reverse engineered, or stored in or introduced into any information storage and retrieval system, in any form or by any means, including photocopying and recording, whether electronic or mechanical, now known or hereinafter invented without permission in writing from the publisher.

Dorrance Publishing Co
585 Alpha Drive
Suite 103
Pittsburgh, PA 15238
Visit our website at www.dorrancebookstore.com

ISBN: 979-8-88925-170-5
eISBN: 979-8-88925-670-0

# PREFACE

There is only one word that can describe my grandpap after delving into thousands of words that he attempted to put forth as an uneducated young man from Czechoslovakia at that time known as the Austrian-Hungarian Empire—"Brilliant!" Grandpap was an unschooled coal miner but highly intelligent to put this story together. With broken English throughout, and a comma utilized after every three or four words, he put together a historic truthful writing of the Pennsylvania coal mines and the families that made this country great in the late nineteenth and early twentieth century.

Growing up as a coal miner's son living in a coal mining town (the patch) assisted me in understanding his notes and story. I tried to keep my grandpap's spoken word, his voice, as close to what he was saying to get the deep feeling on who he was, and how he saw families living in the coal camps. It is simple writing about simple uneducated mining families that were considered at that time the lowest class of people on earth.

As you read this story you will be able to visualize how brutal these coal mining families lived. The families spoken of are real and the daily lives written about actually happened. The names have been changed to keep the innocence of these good industrious people/citizens of this great country.

We constantly are reminded about the difficulties people have in this country, but with food stamps, Medicaid, HUD, and other benefits there is no reason to complain. The coal miners of the nineteenth and twentieth centuries had no government handouts. For pennies they toiled just to survive. Today's American people could not survive in the world of the laborious coal miner.

# I

## THE COAL MINES

The following chapter of this book originates in the mid-1880s and takes place in the coal mining communities in the vast bituminous coal fields of southwestern Pennsylvania. For better and easier understanding, and closer familiarities of the environments and circumstances in and out of the coal mines, the story unfolds chapter by chapter about the men and their families who make their living by mining coal. I will familiarize you briefly and outline the background for you so that you can more easily and with better understanding of the conditions and many circumstances and hardships that surround the miners and their families in the following chapters. You will be acquainted with the coal miners and their families and the entire mining neighborhood.

Let us begin about the coal and the mine, its layout, and the beds of coal, and proceed about the mining of the coal.

The seams or beds of coal lay under the ground from around twenty feet and as deep as six or seven hundred feet. The coal beds or seams are sheltered with topsoil with many different rocks and strata. Therefore, there are three separate ways of getting into the coal seams: referring to the opening of the coal seams. Every opening of the coal seam depends on the deepness of the coal bed. This reference applies mostly to the softness and mining techniques for removal of the bituminous coal. The openings into the coal seams are divided into three different and separate categories, or branches namely, the *drift*, the *slope* and the *shaft*. And each of these three different openings have entirely different consequences and impacts in mining of the coal.

Those openings that are called drift mines are with horizontal openings, which usually are opened at the bottom of the hill and are with extraordinarily little grade or none. In the drift mines, the coal is nearest to the surface, and in many instances, the coal seams run out to the top of the surface soil. And many such mines as the coal is being mined out, the surface soil sags into the mined-out pit.

The slope mines are those with an opening to a certain grade, ranging from a small grade to as steep as 35- or more-degree grades. This also depends on the deepness of the coal seams and the length of the slope.

The shaft mines are those that are opened vertically through the rocks and hard strata directly to the coal seams. The depth of the shafts also differs with ranges from seventy feet and as deep as seven hundred feet and depends on the localities and location of the shaft and depends on the pitches of the coal seams. Some coal seams lay level with the surfaces and some seams pitch to certain grades. The thickness of the coal seams also differs in many localities and range from as low as two and a half feet to as high as nine feet or higher. The coal mines, whether drift, slope or shaft always and must have at least two openings or as many as six and even possibly more, which all run parallel.

The main openings are used for, traveling, conveying the coal, and ventilating the mine. In many instances and different mines, each one of the main headings or openings have a sole purpose. In the shaft mines, men, coal, animals, materials, and other necessary tools are conveyed in and out of the mine by elevators, better known as **cages**. In every shaft mine two cages are erected and hoisted and lowered by means of heavy ropes attached to the cages, and at the top of this shaft tower are two large bull-wheels used for the ropes and are operated by a steam engine which are built opposite of the shaft about seventy-five feet above the ground.

The cages are arranged so that if one of the cages reaches the bottom of the shaft, the other cage simultaneously reaches the top of the shaft tower, thus, while a wagon of coal is being put into the cage on the bottom of the shaft, the other cage at the tower automatically turns halfway and dumps the coal from the wagon into the chute that runs into the coal bin. However, if men or other material are hoisted that are operated by signal systems the cage stops at the level landing. The openings in the mine are driven to a width that a sufficient and ample clearances are allowed for free passages, alongside the pit cars after the tracks are laid. Whenever necessary, timbering supports are used under the roof for safety from falling of the roofs.

The main openings are driven as far as the coal acreage owned by the mine owners or company. Some mines are smaller, and some are quite large, depending on the acreage acquired by one company or individuals. Some mines consist of thousands of acres of coal and reach several miles underground.

From the main openings, other openings are driven and named differently according to the location of the coal seams. In many mines the second opening are called **Flats**, one, two, three etc., some are called Left, Right, Diagonal, North, South, East, and West. Some are given other names. From these flats, other openings are started that are called **Butts**. And from these Butts, final openings are driven, and these are called rooms. The Butts in general are driven three hundred feet apart. This method is almost uniform in most of the mines. There are a few exceptions in some mines, which use several different systems to mine coal....

To give more effective and ample ventilation, crosscuts are driven in the rooms about 75 to 100 feet apart, so the air reaches the greatest efficiency as possible to every man working in the mine. The coal mines are ventilated by power driven fans utilizing steam or electricity. In the time when this story began, all mines used steam-equipped fans and hoists. The air was forced down the air shaft and returned out the hoisting shaft. However, as the years advanced, the coal mines have modernized, and most of the mines have switched to electricity, which better mechanized air ventilation, which reversed the ventilating systems. This improved the fans of the suction system; the air being drawn down the hoisting shaft and returning out through the air shaft.

The air in the coal mines is circulated through the openings where men are working. To give proper and sufficient ventilation, the air is than controlled by erected doors, stoppings and canvas linings. Temporary stoppings are built with canvas and boards, and later as the mines advanced, the stoppings were replaced permanently by non-combustible materials as; bricks, concrete blocks or tiles, and are plastered at least on one side. The stoppings must be strong enough to withhold vibrations and strong reactions from blasting the coal and rocks.

It is required by state law that each and every man working in the mine receive not less than three hundred cubic feet of fresh air per minute to protect the health of the men working in the mine. The air in the mine travels and circulates from opening to opening and as mentioned previously the crosscuts in the rooms were driven to reach as close as possible to every man working. The air then returns through a separate opening directly outside because the air through its movement collects impurities while running its course.

After the openings reach the boundary lines of the coal acreage owned by the company, the mine begins retreating by extracting the coal, which are called **ribs**. While the coal is being mined out, the rocks and heavy strata is laid on supports of timber posts and props. The timber and other supports are extracted by mechanical devices, and then the heavy rocks break off in the area where the coal has been extracted. The rocks fall as high as several hundred feet until it fills itself securely. Some of the rocks are so large they weigh several thousand tons.

The coal being dug and loaded at the beginning of this great coal mining industry was done by only *manpower*. In the eighties and nineties, there were no mechanical methods of mining coal other than by hand, but as the years passed, a cutting machine was invented that was powered by compressed air.

The coal was cut under the bottom of the seam, then holes were drilled about fifteen inches from the roof into the coal as deep as the undercutting. Then the coal was dynamited and then the coal was ready to be loaded by the men into the **pit cars** that were built for only that purpose. The pit cars were always uniform in a mine; for they were pulled by the wagons during this era. A horse or mule or sometimes both were used to haul the pit cars to the men to be loaded and sent to their destination, wherever the destination was located, to the shaft bottom, the bottom of the slope, or even on the tipple of the drift mine.

In a slope mine, the drivers haul their wagons to the bottom of the slope, and from there a rope picked up about thirty wagons at one time and pulled them out on the tipple, and in the same procedure, lowered the empty cars to the drivers so they can be reloaded by the miners. The coal was ready to be loaded into railroad cars for further shipments or wherever coke ovens were erected for making coke. It was then hauled to the ovens by larries or a small engine called a dinkey. In later years, the small engines were abandoned and the larries were electrified, thus eliminating one man for every engine.

Charging car or larry pulled by small locomotive

As the mines advanced, the movement by animals was to slow. The non-gaseous mines were electrified and electric coal cutting machines were used. However, the shafts that were gaseous mines, a compressed air motor and cutting machine had been installed to speed up production. The air motors were urgently necessary to haul the coal to the shaft bottom because the mine openings had advanced rapidly and were distant and hauling the coal several thousand feet to the shaft was too slow of a movement and tiresome for the animals.

When coal mining had just began, in all shaft mines with very few exceptions, only **safety lamps** approved by the state department of mines were used. It was a devastating handicap for the miner with such insufficient light and only to work with a small safety lamp.

"Well, that is the coal mine!" With this brief acquaintance, and a little background about the mine gives you some idea and some understanding about the coal mine. You have a rough and brief sketch of the mine where the men spent their daily lives. With this background about the mine, your imagination can easily adjust for the mining life.

The coal mining industry since its beginning has been fighting hazards existing in the coal mines. The owners of the mines with the state safety agencies as well as the Federal Bureau of Mines, are promoting and practicing safety methods with one aim, to reduce mine accidents and keep fatalities to a minimum.

However, providing the mining industry will exist, accidents and fatalities will occur despite all the precautions taken. It is natural that a few men are more careless than others with their work habits. Therefore, despite all the safety practices and work bulletins, nevertheless, accidents occur every day in coal mines. Limbs, arms, eyes, and lives are being lost in the coal mines every day all year long in the coal mining industry of the USA....

# II

## THE MINER

The coal miner, yes, the coal miner is known all over the world. He is known from coast to coast, from East to West, South to North, to every corner of this entire world. Yes, a coal miner, ***men with black faces, "a mere human worm."***

The coal miner is like an earthly worm who bores small holes into the earth, into the ground, and under the ground. He enters the mine every hour of the day and night, not knowing whether he will ever return to the surface, to his home, and to his family, with limb, or an eye or his life. That is the coal miner.

Many people are not acquainted enough with the coal miner and his mining life. They call him dust eater, underground farmer, and many other hideous names. But the coal miner is a *human worm.*

Indeed, thousands and thousands of them on whom depends the entire country, and the entire world. Also, every industry and all other industrial set-ups from near and far foreign lands depend on the human worm, on the coal miner. Yes, the coal miner mining the ***black diamonds*** as it is known throughout the world.

The coal mining industry is one of the major industries in the United States where thousands of men and women are employed or seeking employment to take care of their families. These men mine coal for commercial, domestic, and exportation for multiple reasons and to keep the world turning.

The coal mining industry began to spread rapidly in the late 1880s, and at that time one of the most and largest producers of coal was the state of Pennsylvania. During this period Pennsylvania produced the finest grade of coke. Several years earlier, the mining of coal in the state of Pennsylvania, about life in and around the coal mines enthusiastically got into the motion picture business with the title of *The Black Fury*, starring Paul Muni. This picture had great popularity over the entire country.

When this story commenced, the mining industry was at its prime as well as it was in its childhood. Mining of coal in the eighties and nineties was to dig and load by hand only. No machinery of any kind was used during this era. The miners dug the coal with steel picks weighing two to six pounds. In later years, the coal was undercut and then blasted. This was the method used of preparing coal for loading and then being transported. This method stirred up considerable amounts of dust. The coal dust as it travels reaches every man working in the mine. There was no escape from the coal dust. As new openings were driven into the solid coal, it accumulates exceptionally large volumes of poisonous gasses which is the most dangerous and most disastrous element for the coal miner.

The coal miner is overly sensitive to weather changes, in the fall and winter and also in the early spring. The seasonal weather changes affect many miners with cold and **grippe**. While laboring in the inner workings of the mine, where it was warmer, the miners sweat and perspire heavily, then travels toward the outer mine where the air current is strong and rapid, which affected the miners with heavy colds. The temperature in the coal mine varies greatly. As the air travels farther into the mine, the temperature increases ranging from forty to fifty degrees. This depends on the distance the air must travel from point A to point B. The air also makes considerable reaction at various times of the season.

In the summer, the air enters the mine where the underground is cooler than the air, as the air enters and travels into cooler places it decreases the air volume. But in the winter, when the air enters the mine, it increases the volume causing the air to be warmer. The air increases and decreases during the different **shift** changes. As men enter the mine in the morning, noon, evening, and midnight, the volumes of warmer and colder air cause grave illness to the miners. The different shifts are necessary due to the specialty of the miner. Miners who work during the day might be working on piece work while a miner on night shift can be working on a tonnage basis. But the mines have become mechanized over the years, which eliminated the piece work.

The coal miner very easily caught colds, and if he does catch cold, the cold in most cases is accompanied by grippe and flu. This causes many days of lost work until he fully recovers.

Miners begin to suffer in their early fifties with miner asthma, which is a dreadful plague if one gets it. The miner's asthma is derived from mining properties such as dust, water, smoke, odors, air drafts, impurities in the air, and many other unknown elements. Those affected with miner's asthma live their remaining days of their life in misery and agony, and constantly gasping for breath shutting off their respiratory system and collapsing the lungs.

It is natural when new mine openings are driven down the grade, and as the openings are developed, they produce considerable volumes of water leading to great difficulty to perfect drainage and pumping, causing the miner's feet to remain constantly wet during his entire working day. The water is cold causing the miner severe health problems. Conditions like this are a contributing factor for many miners with lumbago, rheumatic pain, sciatica, swelling of feet and legs, partial paralysis, and many other chronical illnesses.

Another major difficult problem that develops among the miners is failing eyesight. Some miners in their late forties and early fifties have their eyesight affected due to long hours of darkness beneath the earth. Long hours of darkness in the mines with only a small light on their cap or hip weakens and strains the miner's eyes in their early years. Many of the miners became partially blind in their thirties and could not read without glasses and as age crept up on them, they became completely blind.

Yes, many miners paid the supreme price for mining the coal, the price of a premature end to their good health or life. With this better understanding about the man who mines coal for himself and his family, of the conditions and strange circumstances he deals with daily, I is clear his struggle with life below the earth was an unbearable way to live.

So, let us delve for a while into the Pennsylvania soft coal mining community where our story begins in the late 1880s and get acquainted with the coal miner's family, his everyday life, his struggles, and his happiness. Let us get acquainted with the man who mines coal for a living, and his family. Let us take a peep into his heart, his dreams, his plans, his wishes, his ambitions, and his actions to keep pushing ahead regardless of the ruthless circumstances of daily life. We will learn and see whether his dreams, his plans, his wishes, and his actions remain just dreams and plans or, as for many thousands of them, were led into the graves.

Thousands of miners drifted into their old age penniless at heart, a heart shattered into millions of pieces. Their dreams, their plans, their wishes, and their ambitions turned into an incredibly sad bitter memory.

In the following chapters we will learn and experience how many miners lived a struggling life that was thrown upon them without warning, and many times it was sudden and with great horror. In the upcoming chapters, we will learn what had happened in one community occurring over a half of a century. Although the characters are fictional, the stories are true and such happenings occurred in the poor mining coal patches and coal industry revealing how these communities struggled just to stay alive.

# III

# THE IMMIGRANT LABOR

Coke Oven

Let us venture to Pennsylvania's hilly adjoining counties of Fayette, West-moreland, Washington, Greene, and Alleghany where the mining industry had first developed. Prior to the mining of coal, there was no major industry. Farming and milling were the sole source of income for the occupants in this location of Pennsylvania. A few sawmills could be found here and there scattered with a few farms. Then in the early eighties a coal mine would open and started to serve the local communities consumption. But the last part of the eighties and early nineties, the coal mining industry began its great leap forward with a large-scale expansion. After several years of experimenting and processing, **coke** was perfected, and the mining of coal was secured.

Then, in a few years' time, the mining and coke producing industry developed into a large and important faction, the largest in the world, which onto this day remains the largest mining industry on this planet. In fact, the coal and coke industry began to build other major industrial centers in the United States. By the perfected best grade of coke, steel mills were being erected in many parts of the country until we found ourselves the greatest industrial country in the world.

As time went on, coal mines were being opened rapidly, which in a brief period, a shortage of labor in the mines and with the coke yards became a significant factor. The mine owners and coke yard operators were in despair. With a great demand for coal and coke coupled with a shortage of manpower there was no way ownership could dig coal out of the mines or operate coke yards. During this time, the mine owners were desperate for labor and began searching the entire country for men. A ray of hope for relief of labor came from several immigration centers where thousands of immigrants were arriving daily from the New York harbor known at that time as **"Castle Garden."**

The larger operators of mines and coke yards turned their eyes toward that point for a new and fresh workforce. They owners contacted the employment agencies in New York City for men who were willing and capable. The owners were ready to pay a premium for good able-bodied men. The results were fantastic and highly satisfactory for the owners.

A European mixture of different national varieties, such as English, Irish, Germans, Italians, Poles, Czechs, Slovaks, Russ, Croats, Serbs, Welsh, French, Belgians, Swedes, Scots, Hungarians, and other diverse countries began to arrive at Castle Garden. These national mixtures began to arrive on every incoming train to the coal mining region and the mining communities. Some already had relatives living in the area, some had just friends, but most came from the New York agencies that were promised to the owners.

Some of the immigrants came to the mining fields with the sole purpose and intention to make several hundred dollars and then return to their native land. However, many of them paid for their rich adventure with their own lives as a cause from the inexperience of the hazardous mining industry. They never returned to their loved ones. For those whose fathers, husbands, or sons never returned home, they remained forever only a saddened memory. But their bodies lay in the land of promise, in the land of the free. But an overwhelming majority of these immigrants remained in the land of the free, in America. They made up their minds to adopt and adapt to this good United States for their new home, a new land of promise, their new country so vastly different from their experience in their native land where freedom and equality were never known.

Ninety percent of these immigrants as they settled became an American citizen of their new adopted country by naturalization and became immensely proud loyal citizens of this new country called the United States of America.

# IV

## THE DURANTS

The Durants along with hundreds of others were lured to the coal mining field into the southwestern part of Pennsylvania in the late nineteenth century. The family at once acquired one of the many company-built houses and settled in for good in the mining camp.

The houses were cheaply built with a common frame structure of cheap lumber. The houses consisted of eight rooms designed for two families regardless of the size of the family. The houses were partitioned for two families of four rooms each. Kitchen and a living room on the first floor and two rooms on the second floor, one as a bedroom and the other in most instances was a miner's room where the miners changed their working clothes to and from work. The houses were called **Company Houses.** On the rough ash-covered streets of the mining camp, a hydrant water pump was erected at the center of each street where women of the camp would gather to get their water supplies for their home uses and, most importantly, to gossip, and to exchange the news of what happened around the camp from one day to another.

Syl Durant, in his mid-thirties, obtained work in the mine as a driver. Syl was a jolly young man, carefree and always happy. Syl was a very likeable man in the mine pit and well-liked in the mining community. He acquired many friends in a noticeably brief time through his kindness and wit, and his ever-helping hand to his fellow workers in the mine. Syl quickly learned to jab a word or two of the many foreign tongues, which many times brought the crowd to happy laughter when he began to speak some of the languages.

Among these national mixtures, which have already arrived in this community, we find the Durants, being an ethnicity mixture of an Anglo-Saxon family. The Durants, at that time when they had arrived in the mining community, and when we became acquainted with them, they had four children, and a stork visit was expected in several months. The Durants for some reason or no reason at all liked the letter "J" to be implanted in all their children's names. The fact is all their children's names began with the letter *J.* Jerry, twelve years old; Jenny, nine; Jacky six; and Jane three. With six in the family, the Durants had to spend wisely to meet both ends of their family's needs. Syl worked in the pit as a driver for $1.90 a day for ten to twelve hours a shift. His family needs absorbed all his earnings to the last penny. And if it were not for Dana, Syl's wife, who was very economically astute, the family would have felt the shortages constantly in their daily needs.

The Durants had discussed the situation many times over, but there was no remedy to relieve the economic matter. The entire household burden laid upon Dana's shoulders, and she had to constantly revise the already-stretched budget. It was entirely up to Dana to keep harmony and happiness intact, which was her heart's desire and wish.

Syl Durant learned the mining life in a truly abbreviated time as he grasped the circumstances and the conditions about the mine. Syl learned and found out quickly that working in the coal mine is hazardously difficult and strenuous. Syl Durant began to think hard and, in his thoughts, commenced to plan Jerry's future. Syl had made up his mind that he would not allow Jerry to become a laborious worker in these dreadful mines, to work hard in the pit like he must do daily. Syl began to think that Jerry should get a better education to evade the mine. Jerry was so different and such a fine kid that he should have the opportunity for something better in this world than to be a human worm, a dust eater, a man with a black face, a coal miner. Syl Durant thought Jerry should not waste his life in the coal mine. There must be something better for Jerry. The more Syl thought about Jerry's future, the more serious he became.

Young 14-year-old coal miner

Finally, several weeks later, Syl revealed his dreams, wishes, and thoughts about Jerry to his wife Dana of course. Dana heartily agreed with Syl, and his dreams and wishes would become a reality. What mother would not like to see her son or daughter get a better education? To have better chances in the world for their future.

However, this was only a thought, only a dream, only a wish, and just plans for the Durants. Will their dreams, their plans, their wishes become true one day? Will their dreams and plans be accomplished? One day while Syl was laboring in the mine, a boss had approached him and struck up a conversation for a few minutes.

Suddenly the boss unexpectedly switched to another subject and said, "Syl, I saw your youngster Jerry the other day and he is getting to be a good young fellow. You know, I just thought about that we need a boy in the pit. How about you bring him to work the first of next week?" The boss paused for a moment, as if he would like to hear what Syl would had to say, whether he and his son Jerry could work in the mine together or would he refuse the boss's offer. Before Syl had anything to say, the boss added, "We need a good boy in the pit starting next week. We have opened a new entry into the pit, for which we need a new trapper for the door. "I would rather see your boy get the job. Think it over Syl and let me know as soon as possible so I can decide. Talk it over with your wife, but be sure to let me know."

Syl was surprised. He stood in front of the boss stunned for a moment, as he heard the mine foreman offer a job for his son Jerry. For a moment, Syl emerged into a heavy thought, he was so often thinking of Jerry's future and getting him a better education through more schooling to keep him out of the mine. He wanted something bigger, something better than a coal mining job for the rest of his life.

He saw the boss still standing there and perhaps waiting for a reply, for some kind of answer. The foreman seemed surprised seeing Syl standing in front of him and could not utter a word. Finally, Syl had quickly recovered from the surprise and said, "Yes, sir, yes, sir! That is very thoughtful of you, thank you very much. Yes, I will discuss this with my wife this evening, I will let you know the first thing in the morning. Thank you again, thanks so much, sir."

That very evening Syl and his wife Dana discussed Jerry's future and the offer from his boss as well as the whole family's general circumstances. The decision was hard and somewhat of a heartache for both the parents, but they came to a unanimous decision regarding Jerry's future.

Well, twelve-year-old Jerry Durant went to work in the pit the very following week. Miners cap on his head with an oil lamp on it that looked like it pulled his young head down due to its weight. With a pint of oil in his hip pocket and a hand full of matches in his shirt pocket and a square plug of chewing tobacco peeping out of his other pocket, Jerry now is the newest human worm in the coal mine.

A dinner bucket which almost drags him to the ground, Jerry Durant with a smile on his lips proudly walked for the first time to work into the coal mine. It was the judgment of his parents and that dire need of financial help being necessary, at least temporarily, to send Jerry to the mine.

Thus, Jerry Durant, began his new era in his young life, now at the age of thirteen as a coal miner, as a dust eater, a human worm, a boy with a black face,

Jerry's pay was ninety cents a day, plus the thrill and enjoyment he would experience in the pit among the other men and young boys. At least that is what Jerry thought from the beginning of his mining life, which was too early for him to realize what a miner's life is at the length of thirty, forty, or fifty years old.

Syl Durant and his wife Dana sighed with relief as they thought of the burden that their home needs felt that would be lessened with Jerry's earnings. His help came at a wonderful time of direst need, which had averted poverty in the Durant's home.

A new and happier life began for the Durants. As the days rolled by, the Durant family seemed very content and happy. For a while, the Durants were really one happy family.

The life of the Durants rolled on day by day without any major incidents, except one, a newcomer had arrived to the Durants. Just two weeks old, and everyone in the Durants' home began to love and adore little sister Janis....

Jerry Durant by this time liked his job very much. He liked working in the mine and had lots of talk about his job, about the work in the mine, about the everyday happenings surrounding him. Every day he learned something new, some new experiences he learned day by day; every day was a new adventure for Jerry Durant.

Jerry became an immensely popular young lad among the young and old. Everyone liked Jerry, for he was always a helping hand willing and ready wherever assistance was needed. For that and his innocent fun and wit like his father Syl, he was a very likable young lad.

On one of the evenings, as the entire Durant family assembled around the family table for an enjoyable supper, a conversation broke out amongst the family that the children enjoyed very much when Jerry began his daily routine in the mine. The children popped up so many questions at one time that Jerry could answer them the rest of the evening. So many times, he had regretted that he started talking about his new experiences in the pit. Then the conversation passed onto the happenings in the camp and the entire community and other events that had occurred just recently in the mine and around the mining camp. After the conversation cooled off a little which seemed every subject that was brought up had been carefully discussed, leaving no new subject to discuss or suggestion of something new, Syl then thought that something new has to be brought up to stir up the quietness. After lengthy consideration, Syl spoke.

"You know, Dana dear, I began to think again and very often about Jerry's future. We have already discussed this once before he went into the pit, but I am troubled about our decision." Syl paused for a brief moment, and Dana took the opportunity and said, "Yes, I remember we were talking about sending Jerry to high school. What were you going to say about Jerry?"

"I just wanted to say that Jerry is a very clever young lad. He is quick at any subject and would make an excellent student in a high school." Syl again paused and stared at Dana, watching to see if she is interested in the talk or whether she caught the hints that he was trying to bring into the discussion.

Dana again interrupted Syl and said, "Yes, indeed, I have been watching Jerry also. He is a very smart boy for his age. I sure would like Jerry to get a better and higher education. That is what I was going to say myself. It would be very much advisable and particularly good thing for us to lay some money little by little aside for his education. There is four more months until fall when the school opens, and we can save a few dollars to send him to high school in the fall."

"Yes, we should give him every chance, every opportunity in this world. We should help him. We should give him a start for something better than to be a coal miner, a dust eater." Dana wholeheartedly approved.

Jacky, who had been following the conversation with eager interest quickly interrupted the talk, clasped his hands and spoke with joy. "Oh boy, wouldn't it be great to have a brother as a schoolteacher?" Jacky again clasped his hands as he glanced around the table while the rest of the Durants burst into a laughter. But Jenny, the oldest girl next to Jerry, did not like Jacky's suggestion about Jerry being a schoolteacher.

She hurriedly jumped into the subject, and with serious expression on her face she said, "What, just a teacher? Why not a lawyer or something with a big name like: Jerry Durant Esq?" The house roared with laughter. Little Jane, who was paying attention about what was going on thought that she had the right in the family affairs and that her opinion also should be taken into consideration jumped on a chair so she could be seen, and loudly and with considerable pride she uttered, "or Mr. Doctor!" A happy echo of laughter filled the Durants' home. Everyone in the Durant family was proud of Jerry. They all had sweet dreams about Jerry is proposed and wished future.

With firm determination in Syl and Dana's hearts, they will send Jerry to the approaching school season to high school for a better education. Well, this was only a family discussion as we may find similar chat at any mining family's table.

The following day, the Durants began to check and recheck every single item of needs in their household to resolve and save money until the coming school season which would give Jerry an opportunity to enter the school without further delay.

With determination and sacrifice, that mostly depended on Dana's shoulders to save, she managed to chip little by little for the proposed heartfelt wished school fund. Syl, to help the fund worked many extra hours every week after his daily regular work. Their determination and sacrifice began to show results. The proposed school fund increased, and their wishes may become reality in the near future.

Dana was so happy when she gathered article by article the most first needed things for the beginning of the school year. Just as he would enter the school the coming fall all necessary matters were met. After that Dana had thought that they get along without Jerry's assistance. They made that determination to sacrifice for a better future for their son. Nevertheless, no matter how careful and how secretly the Durants went forward with their plans about Jerry's school, the news somehow leaked out, and in a brief time the whole community knew that Jerry Durant will be going to high school in the coming fall. In these days it was a rarity when a young lad or girl of working-class parents attended high school. A jealousy among the other youngsters of the community began to call Jerry Durant different names and titles: Doctor Jerry, Professor Jerry, Judge Jerry and many other titles. Of course, Jerry did not mind, he just laughed with them and joked with them as usual.

It was the first of August and in only one more month, thirty short days until school starts. Jerry Durant will say goodbye to the coal mine, to his friends young and old, the kids at the camp with whom he grew together, to the adults of the camp who he knew like his own parents. To all, to everyone that likes him, the entire neighborhood.

He will say goodbye to his father and mother. To his brothers and sisters. The entire family will miss him dearly. Yes, the whole community will miss him.

Jerry Durant was such a likeable young lad, that everyone in the mining community wished him luck and enormous success, they were glad when they heard that Jerry will be going to high school. They all wished that he would grow to something better and greater than a coal miner. Everyone in the community felt happiness in their hearts when they heard the news that Jerry will be going to high school.

Thirty more days, yes! But hold on! There are curtains of mystery in life. Nobody can see and look ahead to his or her destiny. If only the Durants could foresee Jerry's destiny because they would be struck with horror and grief.

But God's wisdom sometimes is entirely against human plans, wishes, desires, ambitions, and hopes. It sometimes is best the human's destiny remains hidden and unknown.

The Durants never suspected that Jerry's destiny was cut out from an entirely different pattern than they had planned. Yes, the Durants never suspected that their family happiness in a truly brief time will be marred, and their heartfelt wishes will entirely be destroyed, not of their own fault, but of human designated destiny.

Child coal miners

Meanwhile, as the Durants dream of their sweet wishes, we will pace a street farther and explore the mining camp and get acquainted with more of the neighbors who call the mining camp home.

# V

## THE TARNOWSKIS

In the beginning of the coal mining industry, and when the rush began, many of the national mixtures began to migrate very thickly and some have come directly from the shores of incoming ships straight to the mining fields.

It was early noticed that every individual nationality attempted to group together in a particular quarter of the mining camp and settle as close as they can to obtain dwellings together. Just a street above where we left the Durants, we find a Polish family who just migrated from Poland a few months ago, With the Polish family, several other men have migrated from the New York immigration center and found lodging and board with the Polish family who did not work in the mine, for they could not find room and board with their own people. Among these migrant boarders we find one man named Stanley Tarnowski. A stockily built immigrant from Poland who had arrived several weeks ago. He was alone, but full of plans and dreams rowing in his head about his future. Stanley constantly thought as soon as he made enough money that he would send for his wife Kasha and his eight-year-old daughter, Bronka whom he left behind in Poland with a solemn promise that he would bring them to America as soon as possible.

Stanley was making between $2.00 and $3.00 a day at extremely challenging work in the coal mine. These good American dollars seemed like incredibly good money to Stanley when he calculated the American dollar being exchanged for his native currency. Yes, Stanley calculated that every forty dollars could be exchanged for one hundred Polish Zolty. So, Stanley had decided that working in the mine and making a great wage that it would require about four months before he could send for his family. Stanley Tarnowski impatiently counted the months, the weeks and days before he could save enough money to bring his wife and daughter to this country called America.

Stanley Tarnowski happily pictured his future life with a swirling mind the day he will meet his wife Kasha and his little daughter Bronka at the depot. The time was running too slow for Stanley as he planned the day when this will be accomplished. Yes, his thoughts consistently ran through his mind that they would all have to learn a new language with new and strange surroundings for them. Everything is new and different here, but they will like it here, they will soon learn a new life, new work in this country they called America. Oh yes, all will be well as long as Stanley will have his family here soon. While his family will be on their way, he would find and rent a company house, furnish it with every necessity, and then, yes, he will live happily forever.

This was a sweet dream that Stanley Tarnowski had dreamed every moment of the day and night. And he will dream this dream until his Kasha and his daughter Bronka arrive safely to be with him.

The mine foreman often had sized up Stanley with great admiration. Every time the boss had passed by Stanley's working area, he admired Stanley's broad strong shoulders. The boss noticed that Stanley is strong and heavily built for a young man in his early thirties.

Every mine without exception has working areas that are running down grade or better known as **deeping.** In every place where there is deeping, water accumulates. In some locations where water gathers, the coal still could be loaded. But in some places water accumulates in massive quantities that some kind of drainage was necessary. Pumps are installed in such places to drain the water. However, no matter how sufficient the pumps worked, it was quite difficult to drain the water. The work in such places is more difficult and strenuous than working in dry areas. Thus, a man's feet get soak and wet standing all day long in water. The coal that got soaking wet from the water is heavier, which requires more strength shoveling coal into the pit cars. These kind of places in the mines always give the boss's a headache, for it is difficult to get men to work in wet places despite extra pay being offered to work in horrendous water condition. Yet those places were the most important to mine.

One day as usual, the mine foreman visited Stanley's working area. After the boss's usual procedure of examining the area, to inspect of any danger existing in weak roofs or sides, or whether any accumulation of gas is present, the boss began a difficult conversation with Stanley. The foreman knew that Stanley understood little English, but the boss tried to understand Stanley the best he could.

The boss said, "Stanley, I heard your wife and daughter are coming to be with you from the old country, is that true?" Stanley paused for a while, then gazed into the boss's eyes with a broad smile on his blackened face, as boot black from the coal dust while heavily perspiring as the sweat rolled down his face and his white teeth the only thing visible, his broad naked shoulders almost steaming from digging and shoveling the coal into the pit car. It was evident that it was extremely difficult for Stanley to gather up some words to express himself to the boss. He would rather load ten pit cars of coal than to speak a language that he could not understand. He tried awfully hard and he began to form the words that he wished to speak.

Finally, with great hardship, Stanley uttered, "Sure, me like, me happy, sure." Stanley was glad that he had finished because it was evident that those few words put more sweat on his forehead than the wagon of coal he just loaded.

"Well, that's fine. I am sure glad to hear that," remarked the boss. Then he spoke again. "Say, Stanley! How would you like to make more money? Since your wife and daughter are coming soon, you would need lots of money to set up the home, to buy furniture, clothes, and many other things for the family. I have a place where you can make twice as much money than you are making now. The place got a little water, but strong men like you would hardly notice the difference. What you say, Stanley?"

The boss made a very pleasant impression on Stanley. Twice as much money as he is making now. That sounded great to Stanley. In his mind, quickly as a flash he calculated the money to his native Poland exchange. Stanley could hardly believe that he can make that much money in one day.

Again, he gazed on the mine foreman with amazement, his eyes glittering as a new silver dollar. He was glad that the boss has offered him such a fantastic opportunity to make more money. Again, he spoke with great hardship. "Yes, me like such money, Kasha and Bronka come, must catch everything hurry up. Yes, me like make lots of money. Me go work tomorrow?" Stanley responded in a hurry and waited impatiently for an answer.

"Yes, you bring your tools to my office tonight, and tomorrow morning I will take you to your new workplace. I am sure you will like it. You will make big money in that place," concluded the boss. It seemed that the boss as he was leaving Stanley's work area, was as happy just as Stanley, because the boss knew his worries were over, that he would not have any more difficulties to find someone to work in that wet place.

The next morning Stanley waited eagerly for the boss to arrive. The mine foreman finally appeared and as he finished his morning routine, he took Stanley to his new working area. The water has been accumulating very rapidly despite the pump running constantly. Stanley would have to stand in water most of the day. However, Stanley thought that a little water would not be an obstacle for him. What Stanley was thinking of was the double pay he would receive for a little water he would have to work in all day. He brought himself a pair of rubber boots and began to work in the wet place with much satisfaction. Stanley Tarnowski, young and strong, did not notice any difference in the work, except the double pay he was to receive.

Four weeks later, Stanley borrowed three hundred dollars from his friends and sent the money to Kasha and Bronka for their trip to their new country. Stanley calculated that in two months his wife and daughter will arrive. He will be able to pay back the money he had borrowed, and besides, he would have been able to save a few dollars by the time his wife and daughter arrived.

How happy Stanley Tarnowski was when he stepped out of the steamship agent's office where he had bought tickets for the trip of his wife and daughter. When Stanley got home, he sat down and wrote a long letter to Kasha. In the letter, Stanley gave Kasha full and detailed information for the trip to America.

Stanley instructed her where and how to keep the money. He also warned her of swindlers and false agents.

Two weeks later, Stanley went to the company's office and rented a company house in the Polish quarters of the **patch**. Stanley bought some furniture immediately and other things that were necessary for his family's new home. He then waited for their arrival. Stanley waited for this day impatiently and with great concern. Restless at nights with strange dreams and walking in his sleep were a constant disturbance in Stanley's life.

Stanley began to feel tired after his hard days of work. His red cheeks began to fade a little, but Stanley had plans ahead of himself. *I have to work harder than ever before* was Stanley's thoughts. He has lots of expenses. Furniture to pay for and soon will have his wife and daughter to take care of in a truly fleeting time. He got to settle down first and get a good start with his family. Then later he could take life easier if things would go the way he had planned. Yes! It must work that way, why shouldn't it?

The waited tiresome day finally came. A telegram from the Castle Garden in New York arrived in the company's office where Stanley works stated that his wife and daughter arrived in New York Harbor and they are on their way to Pennsylvania, to the coal fields, to Stanley Tarnowski.

"Finally," Stanley Tarnowski sighed. "Thanks to God, that they have arrived safely and healthy," Stanley Tarnowski whispered to himself as he rushed to dress up in his best clothes that he had to meet his beloved wife and little daughter. Stanley stayed out of work the day before so he can get rested up, but that night he could not sleep a wink.

Early in the morning, long before the train arrived, he rushed to the station, and impatiently paced as he waited for the train's whistle.

The train whistle sounded far away, which was the signal of the approaching incoming train. The peal of the bell on the train was heard closer and closer. The train appeared, hissing of the steam from under the train wheels and in another moment the train will come to a dead stop.

Stanley's heart began to beat harder and quicker. There, in the door of the coach appeared Kasha with bundles in both of her hands, followed closely by Bronka.

"Kasha! Bronka! Moje kochanie," [my love} was Stanley's outcry. A joyful embracing for a moment. What a rejoicing in reuniting to this happy family. Safe! Safe from fear and uncertainty, from tyranny and oppression. Safe under his own care in a new land of freedom, in America.

This were Stanley Tarnowski's thoughts as he saw his wife and his daughter near and close to him. Then, a new home....

The first few weeks were crucial for Kasha and Bronka. New people, new scenery, new surroundings, new habits. Entirely a new change began in their lives. Slowly, Kasha and Bronka began to live life in this new world. Kasha could not imagine a woman's life in America. It is so different from the life in her native Poland. Over in Poland she had to go out early at dawn to the field to do a man-size job. Then when she came home late in the evening, she had to do her housework. What a different world this is, a country called here, America. A heaven compared to her native land. The Tarnowski family settled in the mining camp closely to other Polish immigrants to make their future home here in America, to forget the past, and live to the future.

Stanley worked harder than ever so he could furnish his household completely, and also save a few dollars for unseen or unexpected needs, or just for rainy days in years to come. The following fall, Bronka entered grade school. She had to start over anew. However, Bronka being a clever lass amazed the teacher with her study and picking up the English language. At the end of the school year, Bronka finished very satisfactorily despite the difficulty she had to learn the language. Her teacher was enormously proud of her, and she became an example to other students for her hard study and achievements.

A year later a stork visited the Tarnowski's home, and as they wished, the stork pleased them and left an heir to the Tarnowski's family, a boy of course. The lad was named after his father. However, to be distinct between the two Stanleys, the junior was to be called Stashek, as they used to call the junior in the old country.

Time was marching on. Four years has elapsed without any major incidents at the Tarnowski home. Except we find two more additions to the Tarnowski's family A little lass who was named after her mother came to be, and to be sure which one is mother and which is daughter, the little daughter was called Kashka. After Kashka, another boy came, who was named Juzek.

An ideal family, the Tarnowskis. Two girls and two boys. A real happiness sets in the Tarnowski home. Indeed, they were one happy family. In the meantime, Bronka had finished her grade school. For her ability in the grade school, and the teacher's recommendation for further study, the Tarnowskis were inspired to consider the teacher's recommendation.

Stanley still working in the wet place in the mine, which almost seemed that heavier burden on his shoulders makes him want to work that way because he made more money. Later on, Stanley began to feel really tired after the hard day's work. He did not mind much because he has an incredibly happy family, an incredibly cheerful home. A home that they never would dream of in their native Poland.

Yes, their native Poland. Now it is only sad memories. Many times, they have discussed Poland during their evening hours, as they would read letters from parents and relatives they left behind, thousands of miles away across the sea. They discussed the different living here and their native land. However, the three younger children did not understand what the talk was all about in Poland, except Bronka, she did remember very clearly, and very distinctly the difference between the old country and the new world, America.

Then a problem had arrived at the Tarnowski's home. Bronka's teacher was very fond of her, and extremely optimistic about her studies and her brightness. The teacher had advised the parents and recommended to send Bronka for further studies. The Tarnowskis were enormously proud of their daughter Bronka. They took her teacher's advice seriously and began planning immediately Bronka's future. However, they could not easily arrive on a decision regarding her vocation. Finally, they came to the decision to allow Bronka to decide her own vocation.

The time came closer and closer to the school season. By that time Bronka had decided that she will enter high school first, and later she will decide while attending high school what kind of vocation she will pursue. But something unexpectedly had happened in the Tarnowski's home. An incident that entirely changed the course of life of the Tarnowski's family. The incident also affected Bronka's dreams, plans, and ambition.

While the Tarnowskis and the Durants were preparing their children for a higher education, to fulfill their dreams, their wishes, to plan the future of their talented children who had great ambitions, we will proceed and get acquainted with the other occupants of the entire mining village. To acquaint ourselves with the rest of the community of future Americans.

# VI

## THE NEIGHBORS

As mentioned earlier, the mining camps are built of cheap frame dwellings, consisting mostly of eight rooms two stories high. Every mining camp has a row or two of two or three rooms called **shanties**, which are occupied by bachelors or small families. Many camps consist of fifty to several hundred double houses erected in rows on each side of a layout street. The streets usually are covered with coke ash, which was plentiful in areas where coke was produced.

A small plot of ground running towards an alley is where double shanties and double toilets are built for the use of one of the double houses. The sizes of a plot of ground are different in every mining camp. Some are about 150 long by 40 or 50 feet wide. Some larger and some smaller.

When the mining industry became reality, there was no electricity or running water in the houses. Water hydrant pumps were erected on each street where the people would gather to collect their water supply in water buckets for use in the daily life in their perspective homes. In this particular neighborhood we find the Durants and Tarnowskis living not far from each other. Even though they lived quite close to each other, they were total strangers despite having met many times on the street and at the pump.

In every mining camp without exception, many different nationalities are settled. Nevertheless, the occupants of the camp of many different nationalities met each other many times at the hydrant, in the company store, in church, at social gatherings and many other places. However, when it comes to some celebration, as christenings, weddings, funerals, and holidays, each nationality had their own way of using their traditional habits to celebrate separate occasions in their homeland traditional way.

In those days very few women sailed to this country. It was customary in Europe that first would come the man, then a few years later the wife followed. In thousands of instances, the marital bond ended when the man left his wife behind in the old country. Many a wife never heard, never saw her husband since the day he kissed her goodbye when leaving the homeland. Many children never saw or knew their fathers as their fathers were living and enjoying their new life in this new world. These many men became unfaithful to their wives and children.

On Saturday, early in the morning until late evening, a loaded beer wagon made several deliveries to the camps to help quench the thirst of the industrious miners. From early Saturday evening into the late of night, an echo of music and singing was heard over the entire mining camp. Of course, one could hear different tongues of the diverse nationalities, different songs and music dispersed into the dark and unsilent night.

During Saturday and Sunday, groups of every nationality gathered to exchange the news that they had received from the old country, news from their local relatives. Some were friends and some were relatives.

These gatherings were somewhat of a consolation for their grief struck heavy hearts. Many of them have loved ones far away, thousands of miles across the ocean for whom they still longed.

With similar and often gatherings, the aliens in this strange new country, partly soothed their grief after their homeland and their loved ones they had left behind. These gatherings encouraged them anew in this novel land of promise.

Let us peep into the streets where we can find entirely a different attitude and scenery among the growing generation, the children on the street. There is a new American generation generating from the many national elements. Watching the new growing generation, the new growing America on the streets, in the schools, or wherever you turned, you could have been there assured, that this new generation that was born from these many and different immigrants, will govern this future American destiny.

On any given day you could hear name calling of these various immigrants such as dago, johnny bull, bloody Irish, hunky, and Yankee, but in another minute, you would swear that you hear another different gang. Nevertheless, they were the same children and the same gang you had heard a few minutes ago. You can see them gathered at marble games, at baseball diamonds, flying kites, playing football, playing hopscotch, along with many other American games. Several minutes later you could hear entirely different names, such as Punk, Duce, Doby, Chuppie, Ziggy, Poppy, Robby, Kuppie, Boob, Spooky, Stinky, Hunk, Guenie, Slats, Munk, Muggs, Corney, Buckwheat, Sonny, Cheezie, Mousey, Flunk, Jano, Peesta, and many hundreds more that would fill pages written with these nicknames. Names that you still hear around the loafing places, on the streets, at the schools and even in the workplaces. Many grow old with their popular nicknames.

In this slow, but sure progress, these new generations were being formed of the future and mighty United States of America.

Thus, the population of the mining camps slowly began acquaintances among themselves through the men who worked in the mines, through the children who went to school together, through the gatherings at the company stores, on the streets, across the fences, by the hydrant pumps, in the churches, at social gatherings in tent shows that appeared once in a while during the summer season in the mining camps.

Slowly but surely, the entire camps began to melt into one large national American family. The different national mixture, once totally strangers to one another, began to get interested in each other and began closer acquaintances.

The foreign populations began to learn and speak a few words of their broken English language, and better understanding formed among the different nationalities.

Through their own children, the old folks went to many school parties, school plays, school commencement, school graduations, and many other social and civil gatherings that were sponsored by the community schools and other civil organizations.

The young foreign women who came to this country just a few weeks or a few months ago did not mind taking as many as fifteen borders to help her husband to save a few extra dollars aside in case of dire need, or if they happened to decide to return to their native land. The women were used to hard strenuous work over in their homeland, and coming to this country, they wanted to be useful as they were in their native country. Many young women did not realize from the beginning how hard it was to keep the borders. To wash, to cook and cook. To rise as early as three o'clock in the morning to pack lunch buckets for the borders and prepare the miner's breakfast. Some of the borders worked day shift while others worked night shift, which forced her to be on her feet long hours day and night.

Many young women ruined her early life by overworking herself with too many borders. Many had believed that it was their duty to shelter the men who came to the mining camps daily for work and had no lodging accommodations. Thus, every nationality depended on their own people. However, many women were forced to take borders by their husbands just for greed of the money. Yes, in the good old days, women did not know what a washing machine was; in those days women did not even know what a hand wringer was. The women in these odd and old days did not even know what an electric light was and did not know what running water in the house was. The women could not conceive what an electric iron was and did not know what a soapflake was. The young women had no concept of a sofa. Certainly, they knew not what linoleum on the floor was and for sure they had no idea of silk hosiery.

This was life for the foreign woman in these *good* old days. Many of them struggled as they did in their native land. However, many of them willingly forced themselves to the demanding work for greediness of the money.

This was the neighborhoods in the mining camps at the beginning of the mining industry. A neighborhood of many nationalities that almost consisted of every continent in the world.

Names only Americans could be proud of, such as the Durants, the Tarnowskis, the Berrys, the Hermans, the Leskos, the Marascos, the Farkas, the Marantinis, the Mulligans, the Tedrows, the Nikolajewichs, the Dargeches, the Tarkas, the Polivkas, the Gibsons, the Greenfields, and many others that immigrated to the hundreds of mining camps all over the southwestern coal fields in Pennsylvania.

Some of them arrived directly from the various harbors that landed by ship. Some have arrived from other cities as they have learned from their friends about the coal mines. But mostly, the newcomers were from European countries, and a vast majority were from eastern and central Europe. And today, from these different national mixtures, we see and witness new and loyal citizens of this mighty United States of America.

Today we see these familiar names, however, they are difficult to spell, and even harder to pronounce. Today we see these names everywhere we glance. You can see these names in newspapers and magazines. We see these names as leaders in townships, counties, states, and congress. In low and high places, as prominent figures in American affairs. These names are in business, politics, in religious works, and in every aspect of American life.

Today we hear and see these people near and far across the entire United States, in great metropolises, in large and small towns, and in our own home. Whether it is the smallest community, we see these once European mixture uniting in marriages, disregarding their ancestry and began to live the American way. Choosing their own mates, their own company, their own religion and their own way of living.

Out of these immigrants, new generations germinated in which we see a new and better country to live in, America....

# VII

## DESTROYED AMBITIONS

It was late in August, just a few days remaining left in the month. The sky was clear and blue, and the sun was very bright and its hot and scorching heat was unbearable, and if it were not for the northern breeze that cooled off the heat a little once in a while, it would be extremely difficult to accomplish any type of chore.

It was about three o'clock in the middle of the afternoon. Several women had gathered by the hydrant pump in the middle of the street to get their water supply before the men would return home from work. Nevertheless, the women seemed hurried so they can find enough time for friendly gossip, despite they did rush to the pump as they could not lose a moment of their time with alibi that the supper is not ready on the stove. But in a minute or so everything was forgotten and the gossip developed into an interesting conversation.

The gossiping would continue, who knows for how long; no one knows, if it was not for something that disrupted them suddenly. One of the women happened to glance in the direction of the mine and was attracted by a crowd coming from the mine toward the camp. And as the women saw the crowd coming toward the camp, they suddenly broke up their gossip, picked up their water buckets and rushed towards the approaching crowds.

A group of men followed by children were nearing the camp, and as they neared the camp, more people with children added to the already large crowd.

Four men carried a stretcher getting closer to the camp. The stretcher was covered with a blanket. More people had gathered on the street, and more children closely crowded the men who carried the stretcher as the crowds silently followed them with grief on their faces.

Then one of the youngsters peeped under the blanket, and as being scared, he cried out, "It's Jerry! Jerry Durant."

Dana, Syl Durant's wife, with happiness in her heart just had finished wrapping the last package that Jerry will need for the school in the coming week. "Oh, Jerry darling, finally your opportunity has come. Three more days and you will be on your way, to a better life, better than your father's life in the coal mines." Dana whispered these sweet words as she had laid the last package on the table. Staring at those packages on the table, she sighed with somewhat of a fearful anxiety. Dana then paced toward the window and stared through.

"Oh God, my God! What is that? Someone must have gotten hurt in the mine. They carry someone on a stretcher. They are coming down the street this way. Oh my Lord!" Dana spoke to herself with fear as she saw the crowd nearing down the street closer towards the Durant's home. Dana was about to go out and see what happened, and who is it that got hurt, when the crowds with distress on their faces paused in front of the Durant's home. They brought in Jerry Durant with a broken leg that had been run over by a pit wagon. Dana heard of the accident, seeing Jerry lying on the stretcher, the shock was too great for her, she passed out in front of the crowds.

The company doctor was summoned, but he could do nothing but order Jerry to the nearest hospital. Jerry's leg was crushed so bad by the week's end Jerry had to have his leg amputated right below the knee.

It took six months before Jerry could leave the hospital, minus one leg. Fourteen years old and standing on one leg on the hospital steps with a sad look in his eyes, looking out onto the wide world with a gloomy future.

All hopes for Jerry's future were shattered in a few minutes after years of dreaming and planning. The early adventure in the coal mine was very costly for Jerry Durant.

One year later in the following spring, Jerry Durant appeared for the first time back on the street since he had left the hospital, with a wooden leg attached to his knee. Jerry leaned against a fence post and his thoughts wandered some places unknown to him. His thoughts were aimless and empty. Then he whispered to himself, "Pegy. That is what they are going to call me, yes, Pegy Durant." Jerry sighed heavily. And again, he began to whisper, "Well, I am only a dust eater, just a human worm. Where can a coal miner with a black face? Yes, where can he go?" Jerry's mind wandered as he leaned against the fence, gazing into the dark soil, when he heard a voice behind him saying, "Oh hello Jerry! How good to see you again on the street. I guess it must have been terribly hard for you to lie in the hospital bed for so long." This voice of a familiar girl awakened Jerry from his gloomy thoughts.

"Oh, hello Bronka. Thank you very much for your kindness and your kind words. And thank you again for not evading me on account me being shy of one leg." Jerry spoke the last few words jokingly trying to hide his thoughts and bitterness towards his handicap, which he must face in the future.

"Do not be depressed for the loss of one of your legs, Jerry. If it is God's will, you have to carry the burden. Many thousands carry their burden with a greater handicap than yours. Some are blind; some are totally helpless by the loss of both arms and legs. You have seen them in the hospital. Cheer up, Jerry Durant."

"Bronka, you are an angel. A girl like you will make a fellow forget his worries. I guess that I must get used to my handicap and live with it. Yes, Bronka, I got to think of my future." Jerry's lips show a faint smile for the first time since he left the hospital.

"That is the spirit, Jerry. I realize that your dreams and ambitions are for something better in life have been partly destroyed, but you should not give up all your hopes for your future happiness. There is still a lot of happiness left for you in this world, Jerry."

Jerry feels happier and more content, less self-conscious after he heard Bronka's sweet encouraging words. His eyes have brightened, and Bronka's presence made him forget all his worries. And now his troubled mind seemed cleared. Jerry was once more jolly and an always smiling Jerry Durant.

Then he said, "I heard you were going to nursing school next fall. Is that true, Bronka?" Jerry glanced sideways at Bronka with curiosity.

"Well, I'd like very much to go. I do not wish to spend my life in the mining hole." Bronka paused but regretted she had spoken of that. For she suddenly thought to mentioning of the mining hole would bring Jerry's thoughts to a gloomy mood. Then she tried to mend her former sentence, saying, "Not that I do not like this part of the country, but I want to see more of this beautiful United States, and more important, my wish to help others like you when you were in the hospital. I want to help those in pain and distress, those less fortunate in their lives than we are."

"You have a golden heart, Bronka. I wish you all the luck in the world." Jerry's eyes filled with tears and to hide his emotion, he turned sideways and stared somewhere far beyond.

"Oh, it is only spring. It is a long time to next fall, anything could happen, you know." Bronka sighed and started down to the far street. Jerry gazed the way Bronka disappeared. Yes, he gazed that way for a long, long time. Meeting Bronka seemed that his troubled mind had soothed like a balm on an injured heart. His thoughts wandered somewhere that nobody knows but Jerry.

Then he whispered to himself, "Yes, Bronka, is the nicest girl I ever met. She has a heart of gold; she is an angel. I wish her the best of luck. No, nothing can prevent her wishes, her ambitions. She is too good of a girl."

Thus, Jerry continued to whisper to himself as he still leaned against the fence for a long time after Bronka had left him.

The Tarnowskis had discussed Bronka's nursing education often, and with serious thoughts. They finally have decided to send Bronka to the nearest hospital to start her preparation for ambitious nursing. Her brightness in grade school gave them hope and assurance for her nursing carrier.

However, something unexpected had happened that shattered and destroyed all the dreams and plans for the Tarnowskis and Bronka's wishes and dreams.

Stanley Tarnowski has been working in the mine for a good while and for the last several years he has been working constantly in a very wet area. Stanley has been working in places where water accumulates rapidly. Despite the pumping of the drainage system hourly, it was an insufficient way to get rid of the water. Stanley feet were wet all the time during his working hours, and besides, the work is much more difficult in wet places. The water in the mines is very cold and also consists of many different mineral elements that affect a miner's health eventually. Many miners are affected by this type of work in their early fifties.

After several years of this kind of work, Stanley began to feel weakness in his legs and on numerous occasions extreme pain in his back. Stanley did not think it was serious. He often thought that it was just a little tiredness. However, this tiredness became heavier and heavier until one morning when he got up for work to his surprise he could not stand on his feet. His legs were helpless, he could not stand up.

Stanley stayed out of work that day thinking that all he would need was a good day's rest. He told his wife that challenging work made his legs weak and tired. With a day's rest, he would be ready to go back to work the following morning.

The next day Stanley's legs were slightly worse and he had to stay out of work again. One week had passed and Stanley's legs went from bad to worse. Finally, his wife summoned a doctor.

After a rigid examination by the doctor, he revealed that Stanley's legs below the knees were partially paralyzed. The doctor advised him not to attempt to do anything for at least several weeks and it would be better to stay away from work for even a longer period. The doctor also revealed that his legs became affected from the water in the mine and his daily strenuous work.

The summer days were closing fast and the fall season was approaching very quickly. The Tarnowski's home became more sad each day. The savings that they had put away for the past few years began to vanish fast. There were no other prospects for any other income for the future and Stanley's situation did not change. And all indications were that Stanley would never work in the mine again. The plans for Bronka to start her nursing carrier were put on hold for the coming fall, Kasha, Stanley's faithful wife began to worry, leading to many sleepless nights, thinking of the unpleasant situation that the family had encountered.

All of their earnings were gone. What is she going to do? She must do something, she must find a solution, Kasha thought to herself. Then after several days of thinking and searching for some way out of the situation, Kasha made a profoundly serious decision. A decision that gave her new hope to continue the burden where her husband Stanley left off that she hoped to continue until a ray of sun will shine again on her once-happy family. Soon after, Kasha made her decision to speak to Stanley with soft and encouraging words.

"Stanley, I made up my mind. You may not be able to work as you did in the past. I have decided that we will keep a boarding house, which is the only way we can keep our home from poverty." Kasha spoke these words with firm determination. Stanley realized that his protest he just uttered would not make any changes in her decision. It was hard for incoming immigrants to find lodging and boarding at many mining camps. The companies of the mining camps encouraged many young couples who were willing to work hard to keep boarders. Of course, this would eliminate lots of worries and hardships for the men that seek mining employment, and this would also ease the company's management of hiring miners if they could find satisfactory boarding.

Kasha also foresaw that a boarding house would be the only thing that will prevent disaster to her family. She also realized that in the boarding house that there was demanding work daily ahead, but there was no other alternative to the situation.

Kasha had planned that ten or twelve boarders would keep the Tarnowskis alive and a little happy. Kasha then went to see the superintendent of the camp to let them know her whole dwelling consisting of eight rooms with the intention to make it a boarding house.

The superintendent was more than happy to hear this news and began to send men there the very next day to make the necessary repairs. The mine superintendent offered Kasha the house free of rent just so she would keep the boarding house in the camp. Bronka learned of her mother's decision so she gave up her ambition to become a nurse because she could not leave her mother to work herself into an early grave.

Two weeks later, there were fifteen boarders at the Tarnowski's boarding house. There was a little ray of hope for Bronka. Next year or the year after that, it would not be too late to attend nursing school. No, it would not be late if conditions permitted. Bronka still was hoping that the time would come for her dreams to become reality of becoming a nurse. She planned and hoped that the younger children will soon take her place and help her mother.

Kashka, Stashek, and little Juzek. Yes, they can take her place while she is away. This was Bronka's dream, dream but not reality. Kasha had under-judged the task she had undertaken. Working from the early hours in the morning to the late hours into the night undermined her health quite rapidly. Then the last rays of hope for Bronka were gone. She had to take the helm of the household to save her mother from destruction, from serious illness, or possibly from an early death. Bronka with the other two children had to take care of the much-burdened Tarnowski family.

Two years had passed since the Tarnowskis had been in the boarding business. Stanley was able to walk around a little, but not able to do any arduous work at all. He only could do small errands around the house.

Challenging work in the boarding house affected Bronka also. She began to become pale and weak, losing her appetite and weight. She finally had to consult a doctor. The doctor had discovered a symptom of tuberculosis. The doctor's order was very severe and strict. A long rest in a tuberculin institution. The doctor revealed that there is still hope for a cure and restoration for her health if she left at once for rest in the institution he highly advised. Bronka submitted to her fate calmly with her parents' insistence and the doctor's advice. She realized that it would be best to take the rest.

The whole camp was filled with sadness and grief upon knowing that Bronka Tarnowski had to leave for the institution. She was so polite, so popular and more well-liked than any other person in the camp. Many eyes were filled with tears when they had said their goodbyes to Bronka at the depot.

Also, there was someone else at the station to say goodbye to Bronka Tarnowski, Jerry Durant. He was pacing the ground around the depot impatiently. Only the sound of his wooden leg was heard on the hard ground surrounding the depot.

"Oh, hello, Jerry! Good morning. What are you doing here so early in the morning? Are you waiting for someone."

"I was waiting for you, Bronka," responded Jerry with his face fully blushed and thinking that Bronka would surely disregard him. He thought to himself, *I am just a peg leg anyway.*

"For me, Jerry? Why, I do not understand, Jerry," she quickly intervened.

"You know, Bronka, ever since I've known you, I've always cared for you. You know, Bronka, I have been in love with you secretly, but please do not scold me for that. Oh, please, I know I am a worthless crippled tramp. But believe me, Bronka, I cannot help it."

"Why, Jerry Durant, do not talk like that. You are not a tramp; you are a nice young lad. I've always liked you too."

"Bronka, I promise I will pray to God every night for you and that you would return soon, real soon, Bronka. And believe me, I will be waiting for you, if, if you care, Bronka."

Appearance of the train interrupted further conversation between Jerry and Bronka. She hurriedly grabbed her luggage and ascended the train steps, then she paused on the platform, waving her hand saying goodbye everybody. "I will be seeing you soon. Goodbye, Jerry."

Bronka's last three words gave Jerry Durant somewhat of a new hope and new courage for a future life in the mining camp. She uttered these three words so sweetly with a sweet smile on her lips.

Typical coal mining family

Years later Bronka Tarnowski did recover and returned to her home with her parents in the mining camp. As he promised, Jerry Durant did wait at the little depot for the train on which Bronka arrived.

After years of rest, Bronka recovered her health, but her dreams and ambitions were destroyed forever. Jerry Durant got accustomed to his handicap. With Bronka in his heart, his life again brightened for a new hope about his future. He got back into the pit, back into the coal mine. The company took his handicap case into consideration and gave him work that he could make a living with less hardship. He was given a job that requires less or no walking. He was given a job to operate an underground motor, which of course he was able to ride during his working hours.

Jerry and Bronka understood each other's ways clearly. They understood their dreams and plans, their wishes and ambitions for a better future, for further and better advancement in this world.

After a year, Jerry got settled in his job and felt assured, he would be able to support a wife. Finally, Jerry gathered up enough courage to ask Bronka to marry him. Bronka was certain that her younger brothers and sisters could take her place in the home and realized that her parents were willing to let her go to enjoy the rest of her life and happiness with the man she loved. Her parents felt sorry for her that her beautiful dreams, wishes, and ambitions were so cruelly destroyed by no fault of her own, and no fault of others.

Finally, Jerry and Bronka got engaged to be married. A wedding occurred that the entire camp remembered for a long, long time. The whole camp, the entire community has enthusiastic respect for the couple.

Everyone in the camp felt sorry for the two young souls who dreamed so sweetly about their future, and so suddenly their dreams were destroyed. Yet the community was so happy that these two young people got married.

On their wedding day everyone from the community brought personal gifts. Some gave money, some home furnishings that completely furnished the young couple's household.

Thus, Jerry Durant and Bronka Tarnowski have been united into holy matrimony and began their lives anew. Jerry Durant began his manhood with the sad experiences of being trapped in a coal mine for the rest of his life. Jerry Durant remained just a coal miner, just a dust eater, a human worm, a man with a black face.

# VIII

## FATHER DANIEL

As the population has steadily increased throughout the entire coal mining region, it was certain and desirous that some kind of religious or spiritual guidance was necessary among the vast coal mining people. It is important and necessary to preach the gospel to the different national mixtures with different religious beliefs. The heads of the various religious sects that spiritual guidance was extremely needed before the population of the coal mining region would forget their religious obligations.

One of the first spiritual counselors that arrived at the mining camp was Father Daniel, a Catholic priest. From his appearance, Father Daniel was in his early thirties, but his health was already undermined by hard and strenuous work in the past. Although a young man, it could be plainly seen that a few gray hairs had appeared here and there in Father Daniel's bushy dark hair and wrinkles had started to form on his forehead.

The bishop had chosen Father Daniel and sent him out to the mining region to sow the word of God among the different nationalities, to work among them, to organize a congregation among the distinct groups.

Father Daniel sighed heavily when he received the order, however, as an obedient servant, without complaint, Father Daniel packed his few belongings and departed for his new destination. Fortunate enough that Father

Daniel could speak several foreign languages, which lessened his worries a little when he learned that there were many different nationalities in his new and future field.

With a small traveling bag in one hand and a light suitcase in the other hand, which was all his worldly property, Father Daniel paused at one end of the mining camp.

It was a little after three o'clock in the afternoon in the beginning of September. The sun was well over to its goal towards the west when Father Daniel dropped his suitcase and bag to the ground, pulled his handkerchief out of his pocket and begin wiping heavy perspiration from his forehead glancing around the mining camp. As the children neared the camp, some playing ball on the run, some chasing one another and others playing different games, Father Daniel seemed amused seeing the children running and playing as they drew closer to him. The children approached Father Daniel, seeing his suitcase and small bag on the ground. They began circling Father Daniel with curiosity thinking Father Daniel was a peddler who came to camp to peddle his goods.

Father Daniel glanced at the children and smiled very heartily saying, "Hello, my good children, how have the lessons been today?"

The children began to get friendly with Father Daniel and stepped closer to him and Father Daniel began to ask questions of the children. He pointed his finger at a fourth-grade boy and asked, "What is your name, young fellow?"

"My name is Mulligan, Barney Mulligan," responded the little fellow.

"And what is your name, fellow?" he asked, pointing to another boy.

"My name is Durant."

"And you, young lady, what is your name?" He pointed at the girl who stood by the crowd.

"My name is Kashka Tarnowski," answered the little girl.

Young Barney Mulligan was a fearless lad. As Father Daniel paused for a moment and glanced over the children, Barney stepped a little forward and asked, "Who are you, sir?"

"My name is Father Daniel. I will be seeing you from now on, my good children," softly, with a smile and kindness, Father Daniel explained to this group of young children.

"Mulligan, can you tell me where some Catholic families are living in the camp?" asked Father Daniel.

"Oh yes Father, many Catholic families live here. We are Catholic too," responded Barney proudly.

"We are Catholic too," interrupted Kashka Tarnowski from behind the circling children.

Father Daniel slept that night at the Mulligan's home. The Mulligan's children had to sleep that night on the floor in the room where the men changed their clothes so Father Daniel would have the front room. The following morning, Timothy Mulligan Sr., stayed out of work and went with Father Daniel throughout the camp to acquaint the many Catholic families with Father Daniel as their new priest, the new spiritual counselor.

Mulligan also took Father Daniel to the mine superintendent where he was heartily welcomed. The superintendent at once promised to Father Daniel that he will at once remodel one of the camp houses and turn it into a temporary church, until necessary funds can be raised to build a church to suit the new congregation. He also offered a house for Father Daniel to live in until he finds himself other living quarters.

At least one of the worries that confronted Father Daniel was eased. He had a temporary church and a place to live.

The following Sunday, the Catholics and many non-Catholics heard church services for the very first time at the mining camp. However, it was not very rosy for the new priest to organize the many nationalities of different tongues into one congregation, and furthermore, so many of the Catholic families' religious faith had begun to fade away.

Father Daniel foresaw that difficult and strenuous work lay ahead in this new wild field for him. He knew that the undertaking in this field could not be done overnight. He knew that it would take years of patience and prayer to accomplish his mission. Many of the young children were bad and mischievous and it would take time and patience to bring the youngsters to church to learn real Christianity and lead them on the road to God. Father Daniel immersed himself into deep thoughts as he rested at his small desk after a hard day's work. His thoughts carried him back into his early years, to his school days, to his colleagues who studied with him in his growing years.

Some are doctors, lawyers, and successful businessmen, with wives and families. He compared himself to them. Yes, he was always struggling and toiled at hard work to save souls from evil sowing the word of God among those that were coming to this new country and found no new spiritual coun- selor. His thoughts continued on those who would lose their souls, no one would guide them, warn them from evil, or reach out for their salvation.

With these thoughts in his mind, Father Daniel's heart began to feel at ease. Father Daniel began to fill contentment. He began to fill God's calling to teach these thousands of immigrants. To read the gospel to them, bring greater rewards than just mere worldly luxurious gifts. No, not worldly, but everlasting rewards. With these thoughts lingering on his mind late into the night, he slumped in his chair and dozed off into a sweet deep slumber with two large tears rolling down his cheeks.

Father Daniel remained this way until the following morning hours when he was awakened by a slight motion in the next room. Before Father Daniel got out of his chair and glanced around the room, it was quiet again. As he stepped into the next room, he discovered that the door leading to the street was slightly opened. He did not remember and doubted that he left the door open and yet, the door was open. Father Daniel quickly glanced over the room but could not see anything that was moved or taken, and whoever it was did not have enough time to take anything. Again, Father Daniel glanced over the room. His eyes then stared at the small bag that he brought with him. He just now remembered that the first collection in last Sunday's church service was in the bag. He also noticed that the bag was halfway opened. A cold sweat of large drops appeared on Father Daniel's forehead as he stood and stared at the empty bag. He kneeled down on the floor and opened the bag full and wide. To his astonishment, the collection, the first collection that was taken up dur- ing last Sunday's church services was not there. It was gone! One Hundred and ninety-five dollars was gone!

Father Daniel knelt there for an awfully long time. His hands clasped; his fingers clinched tightly together as he stared at the faded ceiling. He could not cry or curse, for he was a priest. No one would expect a priest to curse. Nevertheless, priests are just flesh and blood as any other human being, but priests have weaknesses; a priest is no superman. He can fall into temptation just as any other human being, as any other person. No, Father Daniel did not curse. But he did not quit. He rose from the floor and walked into the other room where he spent the rest of the night in silent worship. Father Daniel knelt before a large crucifix and silently meditated for hours asking the Almighty for strength and patience for his new and wild neglected field.

Father Daniel had decided that no one person shall know of this bold and daring theft. He also resolved that he would compensate this theft out of his own salary, when or if he would receive any. With contentment in his heart, Father Daniel retired early in the morning for a few hours of rest with hope for a happier and more peaceful life in this strange new home among the diverse nationalities.

Only little over a month since Father Daniel had arrived at the camp, he felt years older. What would happen if the people of his church would demand the money. If the just newly elected church board of trustees would demand the money. What was he to do? He would lose faith with the people of the camp, not just among his own church members, but among the entire camp population. He would be driven away as a thief, a robber. Who would believe him? Nobody!

Father Daniel resolved that he would try to trace the theft, but how could he? He hardly knew the body of the camp in this strange mining community. But one thing he thought, whoever stole the money must have been from this camp and must be well acquainted with the neighborhood and its people. Father Daniel hoped that someday he would uncover the theft or he hoped that the thief himself some day will come to his home and admit and confess of the theft.

Nevertheless, Father Daniel never forgot to pray daily for this person who stole the money, and one day the thief will return to God. And the theft will be forgiven.

# IX

## REV. M. KARIN

Young, energetic and husky, full of hopes and knowledge, Rev. Monitor L. Karin just several months out of the seminary and newly ordained, found himself in the same neighborhood as Father Daniel. The ministerial synod of that district deemed that the coal field with its many surrounding mining camps opening, rapidly, a religious mission was urgent among the different religious occupants in the mining camps and diverse communities.

Rev. Karin was chosen by the synod and sent to the mining camps to preach the gospel to the different faiths other than the Catholics. In the camps where Rev. Karin had arrived were many protestants, Christians, Lutherans, Episcopalians, Methodists, Baptists and many others who Rev. Karin was to preach the word of God. His mission was identical to Father Daniel's. Rev Karin like Father Daniel found nothing but demanding work and worries waiting for him. He hesitated for the first few days about what he should do. He had a thousand notions to give up before he started his mission. He wanted to quit before the first word was spoken. However, he thought of Father Daniel and saw that he began his challenging work without complaint, but with encouragement, that Father Daniel overcame his obstacles with demanding work. The example of Father Daniel quieted Rev. Karin down and he finally decided to stay and try his best to preach the word of God among the different nationalities and faiths.

Rev. Karin like Father Daniel was welcomed by the mine superintendent and was also offered a house as a temporary church and quarters to live in. Well, this was a little encouraging for the Reverend. The mine official realized that religious teaching was very urgent and necessary to the different national mixtures.

Rev. Karin never anticipated the hardships and worries regarding the arduous work in his new endeavor. He never thought that sowing and preaching the word of God, reading the gospel to many others that he would be persecuted, criticized, be scorned, be spat at, disliked, and loved simultaneously. Then Rev. Karin's thoughts ran deeply. He is supposed to be a follower of Christ, to start to preach where Christ left. He then thought that Christ was crowned with thorns and was crucified. This thought gave him a new strength and determination that he would never abandon the field of his mission. He has been honored to be chosen among millions that God called him to be the worker to work the vineyards. Satan's temptations finally vanished, and Rev. Karin resolved that he would preach and read the gospel wherever it may be.

A few weeks later, Rev. Karin and Father Daniel met for the first time in their lives at the little post office. From the appearances, both the ministers seemed worried. Their simple clothes proved that their financial standings were not very generous or promising. A shake of hands and a glance at each other was understood at once of their own circumstances and conditions that they were living. It was not necessary to speak of their hardships; it shown clearly by their appearance.

After a few minutes of conversation about this and that, a likely friendship developed between the two ministers. The conversation then passed on to domestic problems, which led to the people living in the mining camp and their prospective church memberships, however, it had only been a brief time since both the ministers were in the camp.

Both equally had realized and discovered that the youngsters of the camp, especially the boys, were unbelievably bad and constantly mischievous. Both ministers equally realized that something must be done to return the young boys on the road to Christianity and distract them from these mischievous habits.

Even though Rev. Karin and Father Daniel met for the first time in their lives, they felt that they were two remarkably close brothers. Yes, because these two spiritual counselors have the same problems, the same worries and same concerns about the youth of the camp, and to lead the miners and their families on the road to Christianity, on the road to God, could they absorb the responsibility put on their shoulders by their superiors.

The ministers have promised to themselves that they will fight together the evil that is rising very rapidly among the growing generations, the youngsters of the camp, the entire population of the mining camp. A dangerous and delicate problem confronted both of the ministers. Furthermore, they mutually agreed and suggested that they shall meet again and more often in the future. Both ministers thought they should unite in their efforts to check the wrongdoings of the mining camp.

Despite the fact that the two ministers were divided by religious beliefs, they did not see any reason why they could not work together. However, they knew and expected that they would be criticized for their actions by their own church membership. Nevertheless, for the sake to save the children from ruination by keeping a constant check on the youth, they were ready to cooperate as closely as possible, to save the youth of the camp and bring them back to God.

Mining camp minister

It is an old traditional custom among foreign people that whenever there was a wedding or baptism of a child, the occasions were pompously celebrated. Every nationality has their different customs. The customs are traditional that were brought with them from their native land. On such occasions, plenty of baking and cooking were done a week ahead of the celebration. But plenty of liquor covered the tables. Such occasions were celebrated for a week and gave major headaches to mine officials.

In such an event as a wedding, half of the men of the mine and coke yard stayed out of work celebrating such an occasion. Many times, the mine and coke yard had to go idle for several days because the men did not show up for work because of the constant drinking and celebration.

Eventually, a wedding was in the making at the camp. A young foreign couple was to get married. Of course, this wedding was no exception from many others that had been held at the mining camp. However, something had happened during the wedding that created a scandal in the community. At this wedding, the fears of the two ministers were revealed how the youngsters of the camp are not just mischievous, but more on the evil side.

The scandal, however, did not occur in any part of the young couple that were getting married or their parents, but on account of the youngsters.

As the wedding progressed into its climax about midnight, and as the guests entertained by the music and the feast in the hall, a gang of youngsters ranging from six to sixteen years old under a very capable leader broke into the cellar where the liquor was stored. The gang stole an eight-gallon keg of beer and fled with it into the field above the camp. In the field they tapped the keg and then the celebration began among the gang. However, the party who held the wedding never would have discovered the missing beer if it were not for the youngsters themselves. The youngsters could not drink any more of the beer and as they began to stagger, they spilled the rest of the beer from the keg what was left and rolled the empty keg down the hill into the camp. Certainly, the keg created considerable excitement in the camp as the keg crashed through several fences and yards and then knocked down a kitchen door in one of the camp houses. The drunken gang quickly followed the keg into the camp with a great roar. On top of that, the gang created a rumpus of the entire camp.

It was after midnight and people began to return home from the wedding and caught the gang breaking fences and smashing windows, throwing stones at doors causing considerable damage. Some of the young gang could hardly stand on their two feet any longer because the alcohol began to show its strength and the boys became overpowered by the beer. One by one the boys dozed off on the porches, steps and in the streets and into the darkness of the morning night.

The following morning some of the youngsters were questioned about the drinking party. After the quizzing, some of the younger boys broke down and admitted to their parents that they stole the beer. However, there were no prosecutions or punishments on the boys or their parents, but all eyes of the adults in the camp turned to the two ministers hoping that they could prevent further occurrences similar to the one that just happened.

The gang's mischiefs were going from bad to worse. Increased complaints were heard about the gang's stealing, destroying, and damaging, others property. These problems were heard daily as the people became restless about the gang's doings. The complaints were now being directed to their respective ministers.

A week later, after the wedding occurrence, Rev. Karin and Father Daniel met again at the little post office. They heard about the stolen beer and the mischief aftermath. Both were concerned about the situation. As their conversation went further, Father Daniel remarked, "I think we should do something about the situation regarding the gang. We should find out about the gang's leader and break this gang up."

"Very good idea, Father Daniel. But how? What can we do? There are just the two of us and it would be a hard nut to crack, Father Daniel," replied Rev. Karin.

"Well, we must think of something that will distract the gang from these awful deeds. I know it is hard work, but we must do something. And save us also." Father Daniel paused as if he would search for some kind of solution to his words, then he continued. "More and more complaints coming every day. The people are now beginning to think that it is our duties to check the pranks and mischiefs around the camp before it develops into real gangsterism and major crimes."

Rev. Karin just stood there shaking his head and shoulders for he did not know what could be done to solve this consistent problem and stop the gang. Then he quickly suggested, "How about some sort of sports? Baseball, football, or basketball? Something that will occupy their minds."

Father Daniel stared at Rev. Karin than shouted, "Yes, that is right, little by little we may be able to break up this gang and maybe discover who is their leader."

"To do that we must have full cooperation from the school heads and all the teachers. From the parents, and most of all from the public," suggested Rev. Karin.

"I am sure that the school supervisors and the entire teaching personnel will support our efforts. But we shall go to them and put our plans and whole situation to them," explained Father Daniel, and he further added, "I am positively certain that they will wholeheartedly approve of our plans," insisted Father Daniel.

"Say! How about Dr. Graymore? We should consult him. He is a great sport lover. He may be a great assistance to this cause," quickly suggested Rev. Karin.

"That is right! Dr. Graymore is a knowledgeable sportsman, and almost certainly will give us his helping hand," concluded Father Daniel.

Rev. Karin and Father Daniel unanimously agreed that they will visit Dr. Graymore and they would ask him to give his support and cooperation in this grave matter of gangsterism. The two ministers parted that particular day with some easiness and hopes that their first effort toward this plan will succeed and that in time will break up the evil that is spreading among the youngsters in the mining camp.

For both of the ministers have frequent callers at their respected homes from various people of the camp with many complaints about the growing evil around the vicinity. Rev. Karin and Father Daniel were counting on Dr. Graymore for at least moral support in their effort to curb the evil deeds and bring the youngsters back to Christianity. Both of them that night spent many hours in prayer asking the Lord to give them the wisdom and strength to overcome their hardships and to grant them grace to achieve their wishes and plans. To help them save the souls of the innocent children and bring them back to God and decent American society.

The two ministers retired that night happier, with contentment and peace in their hearts and a slight smile on their lips as they slumbered away late into the night.

# X

## DR. GRAYMORE

Dr. R. B. Graymore, young and energetic, full of life, just had finished his internship at one of the largest state hospitals. Upon completion of his internship, he was invited by one of the mining companies to become a company doctor. The mining company was the one where we already find Rev. Karin and Father Daniel. Dr. Graymore accepted the company's invitation and arrived at the mining camp.

Although Dr. Graymore was a company doctor, this did not affect his private medical practice outside of the company's obligation.

At the camp, the miners and their families were under Dr. Graymore's care. Each miner had a monthly fee cut from his pay for Dr. Graymore's medical attention. However, Dr. Graymore was not responsible, and not compelled to take care of operations or confinement cases. Those were private cases and not included in the company's medical attention and agreement.

His duties with the company were to attend miners or coke workers when they received injuries in or about the mine or coke yard, and women and children in the camp to treat common illness. Whatever time he had aside from his duties as a company doctor, he set up private hours in his office to take personal calls around the mining community.

The company provided Dr. Graymore an entire eight-room house that served him for his living quarters and office. The house was rebuilt for his purposes.

Dr. Graymore was a jolly young man. Happy and always smiling. Yet a bachelor, he had one of the women from the camp to clean his office and his rooms, and to prepare him one meal a day.

The children of the camp knew Dr. Graymore from a distance at first. Then kids from the camp knew him as the candy man. Every time Dr. Graymore had appeared in the camp streets, the children would run out into the streets and surround him or follow him all over the camp. The good doctor always opened his little satchel while the youngsters lined up to receive candy from the doctor. At every gate where he saw children playing, Dr. Graymore would pause and join them in their games or begin a conversation with the kids. However, the older children soon would catch up with Dr. Graymore but refused to accept any candy from him. A reaction and funny feeling occurred with the older children and Dr. Graymore's system of dolling out candy to the young ones. The older children began to smell castor oil in these sweetened candy-like pills.

Dr. Graymore did not have a rosy life at the mining camp. However, he was more fortunate and more certain of his surroundings then Rev. Karin or Father Daniel. He was certain of his monthly salary from the company, but the two ministers were not certain from day to day whether they would have any money to buy their meals.

Dr. Graymore's beginnings were hard and slow. It took time before he became well acquainted with the people around the community. He then had to prove to the people that he was a good doctor. He had to meet diverse nationalities and many of the foreign people were quite superstitious about life in general and especially about medicine. Dr. Graymore had a thorny road to climb before he would become a successful and trustworthy doctor in the camp.

His practicing of medicine would be ruined forever at least in that community if someone would die under Dr. Graymore's care in the camp. He would never be allowed to appear on the camp streets again. However, he was a lucky man that no one ever did die during his crucial beginning days of treating the injured or ill miners and families.

Apparently, his financial standing at that time didn't warrant him that he may get married in the near future and settle down in the mining camp. With the progress he was making at that time, Dr. Graymore calculated that he wouldn't be able to get married for another two or three years.

During his stay at the camp, he made only a few acquaintances of the common people of the camp. But he did strike up a friendship with Father Daniel and Rev. Karin. It appeared that the doctor was on the same mission as the two ministers trying to befriend and help the men who worked under the ground hundreds of feet, like a worm, digging and creeping farther and deeper.

For this Dr. Graymore perhaps turned down many offers and invitations to famous clinics or experimental centers from which he could have become a world-famous specialist or scientist. But the doctor was more interested in the simple human being. He was very much interested in the man working in the coal mine deep in the ground, and his family who merely exist in the forgotten mining fields as the entire world looked down on them as the lowest type of human beings.

Yes, this was Dr. Graymore who came to the mining community to study, to help and promote the conditions in and around the mining camps. Dr. Graymore became the living soul of the miners and their families to whom he devoted his entire life. This was his happiness, to stop on the camp streets and chat with the men and women and play with the children.

Dr. Graymore knew them all. And they knew him. Nobody could take Dr. Graymore away from the common good-hearted people, the coal miners, the human worms, the men with black faces.

# XI

## THE MARANTINIS

Angelo Marantini immigrated from Italy as thousands of others who were lured by the coal field, to the coal mines in southwestern Pennsylvania. Angelo settled in the community where we find the Durants and Tarnowskis.

In a years' time, Angelo's family followed him and immigrated to the United States. Nina, Angelo's wife brought her four children with her from Italy and settled in the camp. Nicky, the oldest boy in the Marantini household, followed by Dominico. For short they called him Don. Angelina came after Don and the youngest in the Marantini family was Nanita.

As thousands of miners settled in the coal mines, every miner, every individual seemed that after everyone became acquainted with the mine and the various workings of the mine, they all found their specialty of the type of work they wanted to perform in the mine. Some just liked to dig coal, some liked to work the night shift.

Angelo Marantini opined that digging coal was awfully hard work and he would prefer work that was not so strenuous. He preferred work that was classified as day work where got paid by the day, and to Angelo, the work seemed not so hard as digging coal. But work by the day pays less money.

So, if a man digs and loads coal, he works harder and makes more money than the day worker.

Marantini thought that as soon as he would learn a little about the mine and a few words of English, he would ask the boss for a chance for a better job.

For some reason Angelo always liked explosives ever since his childhood. He was interested wherever shootings were happening in the coal mining industry. Since the beginning of the mining, management employed men called a **shot firer**. He was to blast the coal or rock in the mine. The shot firer had to be a very competent man to perform this kind of work. As soon as Angelo Marantini felt that he could perform the work as a shot firer, he would apply for the job. That was Angelo's constant wish and thought. The foreman promised Angelo that as soon as an opening would come about, he would give Angelo a trial.

Acting as a shot firer in not as strenuous, but a more dangerous and hazardous work. A person working as a shot firer must work with the greatest precaution and must be constantly aware of his duties. A shot fire must spend most of his working hours in smoke resulting from the blast of powder odor or dynamite, which affected many shot firers health.

Several weeks later, Angelo was hired as a shot firer. He was an incredibly happy man with this type of work. The mine foreman felt that Angelo performed his duties in a very satisfactorily manner. Angelo was an honest and loyal employee that any boss would be happy to have under his supervision.

Meanwhile, the Marantinis were visited by the stork. being a formal visit, he left a gift at the Marantini home, a little girl. The little lass was named Pepita. Now Nina had an edge over Angelo. Many times, she said that the house has the majority on her side, and of course, the majority rules.

In the meantime, Nicky was nearing his fifteenth birthday when he obtained a job in the pit as a pit car oiler. His duty was to grease the pit cars wheels when they were not moving. Nicky liked his new job and for the first days he could not keep his mouth closed about his new job. At the supper table he repeatedly explained to the younger kids what he did and how he did it and when he did it. While eating dinner he tried to demonstrate his work. He would grab a soup ladle, explain to the kids that it was an oil pump, then he would bend over to the table leg and try to illustrate that it was a pit car wheel. At the end of the demonstration, Nina was the victim of the demonstration, because she had to mop up the soup from the floor that Nicky had spilled from his demonstrations.

After the demonstration was over, Nicky felt like a hero as the kids stared at him with admiration. Angelo than warned Nicky to be careful always at his work and do not do something that may cause him harm. Nicky just laughed it off. He knew all about his work and needed no advice from his father.

Once in a while Angelo's mind sparked with an idea. He began to think that a little business on the side would not hurt if he and Nicky could work in the mine for a while to save up a little cash for this venture. He felt that Nina and the other children could take care of the little business.

Later on, about a month or so, Angelo confidentially disclosed his dreams to his wife Nina. However, Angelo just regarded it as a dream and a hope. Nina knew that businesses, no matter how small would bring more burden and more worries upon her shoulders. A business surely would require more of her time, and the entire responsibility for the business would require her to reduce her budget to save enough money to start the business.

Yes, a business, no matter how small that it may be would require some immediate capital that the Marantinis did not have. But was mostly need for the business was a location. Nina scrutinized the idea at length. Her expression indicated fearfulness. She thought to herself that a business at this time would be disastrous for the entire family.

Finally, Angelo decided to look around for a location for his business that he had in mind. To his surprise, he did locate a very suitable site which would be ideal for a small business. Just on the outskirts of the mining camp which would be an appropriate location. Just the place he had planned for, that his heart desired ever since he arrived in this country.

A month later, the Marantinis bought an acre of land on the outskirts of the mining village. They had saved enough money to make a first payment on the parcel of ground. And month by month the Marantinis paid the balance for the plot. Angelo sighed in joyfully as he made the final payment on the land.

But to the Marantinis great surprise and sad disappointment, after the deed had been legally transferred and delivered to them, they discovered that all the surrounding land over laying the purchased underground land was owned by the coal companies and they have the reserved rights and that no business establishments shall be permitted on the grounds overlaying the coal.

The Marantinis have paid several hundred dollars for the small plot of ground, and then discovering the reservations the mining company had. It was worthless to them. This worthless deal broke Angelo's heart. So many sacrifices the family had made to buy this place. Mostly Nina, she had to chip here and there to save and make a payment on time. And now, what have they got? The only use they can make of this place was to build a home there and live in it. But when and how can Angelo make enough money to build a home and live there. Angelo's sweet dream for a little business of his own was gone forever. Yes, the Marantinis have heavy hearts slowly begin to forget their dreams and hopes for the future.

However, the Marantinis never gave up. They always dreamed that something, some day will come up into their alley. They hoped that luck would smile upon them some day in the future. They never gave up one moment of their hopes.

There was a ray of hope in the Marantini's home. Nicky, the oldest boy in the family has a beautiful tenor voice. With the proper training of his voice, Nicky could have a chance as a singer. However, it was impossible even to think of such a thing as taking singing lessons. The Marantinis were quite poor and all their earnings were consumed by the family's needs. Since they put every loose penny into the plot of land, they could not save any money. Despite Nina's careful spending and being very economical, there was very little chance to send Nicky for singing lessons.

Nicky loved to sing. Everywhere he went, to his work, on the streets or at home, Nicky always would be singing. His parents were shadowed with grief that they could not afford to give Nicky an opportunity to culture his beautiful singing voice. But they still dreamed and hoped.

A possibility came to Angelo's mind. When Don, the younger son began to work, perhaps then they are able, yes, it will be possible to send Nicky to hone up his tenor voice. Those were the dreams of the Marantini family, hoping that as soon as Don would begin to work, then maybe they can achieve Nicky's ambition.

A company store

Don also has a talent and ambition. Don always loved to play an accordion. Once an unexpected opportunity came to Don's way when a neighbor, a miner decided to leave the camp for his native land and had a small cheap accordion. Angelo bought the accordion for Don for three dollars. Don would practice constantly until he could afford to buy a new one. However, this did not help Don much. To be a good accordionist he would have to find someone to give him instructions. He needed to learn the notes of the music. He needed to find himself a teacher if he wanted to become successful accordionist. The Marantinis just could not afford music instructions.

But Don had his dreams. He thought as soon as he started to work, which would be in the mines, he would save enough money to go to some bigger city and find work and at night he would enter some musical school.

Thean there was Angelina, the girl who followed Don in age. She always wished that she could become a schoolteacher, a grade schoolteacher. What a beautiful dream, and heartful ambitions in the Marantini family.

Angelina was to go to work as soon as she finishes her grades in public school and saved enough money for her to enter a teacher's college.

It was evident that these dreams, these plans, these hopes, somehow retained a happy contention in the Marantini's household. These three ambitious children acquired another musical instrument, a banjo on which Angelini began practicing. Finally, Angelina learned enough that she could play any tune by heart. Later on, they acquired a guitar for Nicky and in a short time the trio had set up a little orchestra. That is just in the home and in the yard, on the front porch or in the family's parlor.

After a short while, they were encouraged by the camp's folk and began to get invitations to play for parties, weddings, christenings and other affairs around the camp.

Of course, there was no compensation for their musical services when they were invited to play. But plenty of eats, and if they cared to drink, they would drink. But that is all they would receive.

At the camp they were known as the Marantini Trio. From the beginning they would just play for their own nationality, the Italians. But later on, they had developed into an immensely popular trio all over the community. Their music was sweet. An accordion, banjo, and guitar. And Nicky was the soloist. They began to make a few dollars a week for their services of music.

It is an old proverb saying, "The sun shines very bright before an approach of dark clouds, followed by a storm." This proverb must have been cut out for the Marantinis, the happiest family in the whole camp, or the whole community. For there were dark clouds nearing with slow but sure approach to the Marantini's household. Behind a shadow, beyond the dark clouds, a disaster was stealthy as a thief nearing the Marantini's home. While the Marantinis were very content and happy with the sweetest dreams and plans for the future, a shadow of sorrow and sadness was creeping up at the family's threshold.

Coke workers, father and son

One day in the early spring, Angelo Marantini came home from his daily work with great joy and a wide smile on his lips. As soon as he entered the house, he eyed Nina. He then joyfully outcried with a large grin on his face and said, "Nina, Nina, I got news for you. Good news for all of us. Dominice got a job in the mine! The boss told me to bring Don to work next week." Angelo Marantini glanced around his family and saw a smile on everyone's lips.

Nina clanged her hands together and whispered, "O Dio, Gracia, gracia!" Joy and happiness prevailed in the Marantini's home.

Now, now it may be a possibility to save a few dollars for Nicky's, Don's and Angelina's educations. Nina weighed the possibility and very carefully thinking she may be able to chip little by little towards her future if nothing unforeseen would happen. One thing she was certain, that it would be an extra expense for Nina. But for Nina, an unexpected call from the stork was on its way.

Fear had set in that something awful would happen pursued Nina often, in fact, constantly. However, she did not confirm her fear to anyone.

Miner's daughters

The following Monday after Angelo brought the good news home, Don started to work in the pit. He started his new job working with Nicky, to oil the pit cars. Nicky was to break Don in on his new job and then Nicky would be moved to another job in the mine.

Oiling the pit cars was to be done while the wagons were at a standstill. As the wagons were being dumped of coal, they moved slowly to make room for those being dumped. The track was somewhat of a storage for the empty cars which were gathered by the drivers and delivered to the men in the workings. The wagons were moving slowly while Nicky attempted to oil one of the moving cars. Somehow, his feet tripped and he fell. His hand fell on the rail and the moving wagon ran over the palm of his hand and cut off all four fingers completely beyond the first joints.

Nicky Marantini, just a little over sixteen, lost all his fingers on his left hand. The dreams and plans of the Marantini Trio plans for the future were shadowed by Nicky's accident.

The women of the camp gathered as usual by custom at the water hydrant pump and began their daily gossiping. Some had come out of the house for water after an early breakfast, and this was now late afternoon. Some women were still discussing the camp's happenings. Some were afraid they would miss something.

Among the discussions was Nicky Marantini's accident which was of particular interest. It was a week after Nicky's accident as this particular discussion took place.

As the women were into their most interesting gossip, a woman at a distance appeared at the other end of the street, and it was evident that she was rushing toward them. It could be seen from afar as she was hurriedly approaching that her face was ghastly white.

As soon as she approached the crowd semi whispering an outcry, "Oh my God," she sighed catching her breath. Then she again uttered, "Oh my God, know what happened? Angelo Marantini got shot in the mine." The woman who brought the horrible news cannot say anything for a moment. Obviously fear and panic had overtaken her. She glanced again over the crowd and by that time all were stricken with horror. Then all in chorus half whispered with tears in their eyes, "My God."

"What luck the Marantinis have. Last week Nicky got all his fingers cut off and now his father got shot by the mine blast. Wonder how bad?" One of the women inquired after moments pause "They do not know yet; He is still in the mine. They just sent word to his family," responded the woman who just brought the news. Yes, we wonder how bad Marantini's accident was? Horrible, complete loss of both of his eyes. The explosion from the hole that he attempted to prepare for charge, exploded with terrific force into his face. The forceful burning explosives penetrated his flesh deeply into his face. The result was that his face would remain black spotted for the rest of his life. However, Angelo did not know and did not care that his eyesight was gone forever.

The dreams, the plans, the hopes, the wishes, the ambitions of Nicky, Don, and Angelina were vanishing rapidly from the once happy and gay family, gone forever. The opportunity which almost was once in reach for the talented three children now were greatly disappointed, hearts broken. Their destiny was sudden, cruel and merciless.

To this pitiful and already burdened Marantini family while Angelo and Nicky lay in the hospital, twins were born to the poverty-stricken family. Greater worries and more responsibility were added to Nina.

As Nina lay in bed, she stared at the two just a few days born twins as tears rolled down her cheeks and began to sob with deep emotion than whispered, "Why were you two ever born? Why two?" Then she paused a moment. A terrible storm came to her mind. A question hurriedly came upon her. "Why were you born? Did your parents welcome you the same way you welcome you innocent twins? NO, I have no rights to unwelcome them. I should be happy that I brought two little angels into this world. Their destiny is already assigned. Oh Lord, forgive me."

Thus, the dreams have come to an end for the ambitious Marantini children. Nicky sighed when he left the hospital, "Fisty, yes Fisty, that is what they will call me. Well, I am only a coal miner, only a dust eater, just a mere human worm."

# XII

## THE NAGYS

Louis Nagy immigrated from Hungary with the destination to the coal mines of Southwestern Pennsylvania. With a few close friends of Louis who also immigrated to the United Stated not quite a year ago, Louis obtained their addresses and arrived straight from New York to his friends to the soft coal mines of Pennsylvania.

After several days of rest, louis friends attempted him to come and work in the mines. Louis is afraid of the pits, saying, ""he would go if the mine would have windows so he can see outside." Well, some mines do have windows. Mines that are called Drift. There are locations where coal crops out to the surface and men could see daylight or get outside through the fall-in holes. Despite all the encouragement Louis friends gave him, he decided to get a job in the coke yards because it was less hazardous than the coal pits.

Louis Nagy settled down in the camp as a coke drawer. Louis came from an agricultural country where he worked as a farm hand. But drawing coke was something new for louis and he had become disgusted with his work that he was ready to quite when he would have enough money and go back to good old Hungary.

Nevertheless, Louis finally broke himself into the new job. And little by little he began to like the work. Several months later, Louis became one of the best workers in the coke yard. Louis was quiet and dependable and also obedient. For his attitude, the boss liked him. Louis also never refused to do any kind of work. If the boss asked him to do some tasks, regardless of if the work were hard or light, dirty or good, he would do it without hesitation.

A year later, Louis family arrived in America, Lizza, Louis wife, brought four children with her. Stevey eight, Georgey six, Charley and Lika two years of age. Louis Nagy was in his early thirties and his wife Lizza was in her late twenties. They settled in the camp close to their friends, so as they say, "wouldn't be so lonesome."

Each coke drawer was assigned to a set of coke ovens from which the coke drawers pull out the coke daily. Every man according to his ability and mainly to his own strength were given as many as four to six ovens in a row called the set. They pull coke out of every other oven each day. The coke drawers were paid by the ovens. The more ovens where the coke was pulled out the more money he made.

Of course, some men were satisfied with two ovens per day, but some pull as many as four a day. Some of the foreigners came to this country with certain intentions, to make money as quickly as they could and then return to their native land to rebuild, to purchase and to improve their standing in their hometown.

The drawing of coke began at midnight or a little sooner and lasted to noon the next day.

Many of the immigrants from east and central Europe brought from their homes and respective homelands a custom, which they thought that their customs will work here in America just as the customs worked in Europe. Over there, wherever they came from in their native lands, the children were used to work and help in the fields and around the home from an early ager. In fact, they began to work before they entered school. Many foreigners thought that it would be helpful if the wife and their children would come to the coke yard and help around the ovens. To them, it was an excellent idea. That way they can get a few more ovens and make an extra few dollars a day and much more.

It started from the beginning, one or two men brought their wives and children to the coke yards which proved extremely helpful. Others saw this, became jealous, and remarked. "If they can bring their wives and children, why can't I?"

In a few months, this epidemic spread over the coke yards as mushrooms spread after a September rain. In the early morning hours, one could see children roaming, hundreds of them at the coke yards. The younger children that could not do hard work were assigned to watering the ovens. Women and older children were forking the coke into wheelbarrows. Some even attempted to wheel the barrows to the railroad cars. Whenever an uproar was heard in the coke yard, it was a woman who tried to push the wheelbarrow, but the barrow was upset as she tried to pull it down the tracks.

Some men used their family for the greed of money, some did just because others did it, and others with the idea it would get their children use to work. But whatever their alibis were, the foreigners did not use good judgement about using their children as miniature slaves.

However, the parents of these children did not realize that the few dollars gained could and would have a greater loss in their later years. They did not realize then that this labor thrust upon their children would undermine their health, and deprive them of the most precious item, their education.

In those days when the United States evolved to the greatest and largest industrial country in the world, with a population constantly growing, including the coal mines, did not include education as an essential means for future life preparation. This opinion prevailed among the incoming immigrants. And this opinion applied correctly to the Nagys. Louis saw that others around him in the coke yards get a great deal of help from their wives and children. Why not him?

It was Lizza who encouraged Louis to take two more ovens every day, and she and Stevey would come down the yard early every morning to assist him as other families do. This would bring according to her calculations about ten or twelve dollars in his pay envelope. This meant a lot of money during these days.

The majority, ninety percent of the immigrants never saw or have earned as much money as they can earn when they arrived in this country. This caused a desire for more and more money and then return to their homeland. Even if they would have to sacrifice their own children.

Many had plans to save enough money and return to their native land and buy a farm or a home, some to brag how much money they have saved. Over in their native homeland, they toil just to survive, but when they arrived in this country, they begin to earn big money with a desire to earn more money. This money greed tempted many foreigners to labor in the coal mines.

Child mine workers

A new life began for the Nagys. Louis went to the yard at midnight and a few hours later, Lizza and Stevey followed to help Louis with the ovens. Stevey's job was watering the coke ovens and Lizza helped Louis to fork the coke into the wheelbarrow. Imagine a nine-year-old lad standing by the coke ovens despite the weather. Cold or hot, rain or snow, Stevey Nagy half asleep on his feet helping his father to make a few extra dollars.

About six in the morning, Stevey was rushed back home to get a couple hours sleep before his time to go to school. What a rest? And so much sleep! Six-thirty to bed and two hours later he had to get up and go to school. No food, not a proper meal before he left because his mother was still engaged in the coke yard. She never had time to prepare a proper meal for her children.

Stevey Nagy was a bright lad from the very beginning. Stevey was top in his class, but later on when he had to venture early in the morning to the coke ovens and do a man's job, he began dropping to the bottom of his class. The strain from lack of sleep and insufficient rest began to have an effect on Stevey's studies. Stevey began to have a difficult time in school. Most of the time he spent in school was sleeping. Under the circumstances of lack of sleep, his good marks in school began to drop, and by the end of the school year Stevey could not make the grade to move on to a higher class. In those days it was automatic to remain in the same grade for the next school term.

The teacher knowing Stevey's abilities in the classroom if he were able to do his studies, would be leading his class again. The teacher had pity on Stevey's condition, and he resolved that he would try to induce his parents about the importance of his studies. The teacher sent several notes to Stevey's parents with the intention that his parents would realize that they are making a severe mistake on forcing their child into the coke ovens. The Nagys just laughed off the teacher's notes, and Louis bluntly remarked, "Why, if I can draw coke, then why my children cannot? They do not need any education to draw coke."

Thus, Stevey Nagy remained in the third grade for several years. And upon reaching his sixteenth birthday, he left school to get a job in the coke yard. Stevey Nagy got his job in the coke yard to haul ashes away from the ovens with a one-horse cart.

As far as we have advanced with the Nagys, I never mentioned anything about their dreams and ambitions in the Nagy family. However, after Stevey began to work, he began to have difficulty in thinking clearly and thus, his mind developed quit slowly. However, after Stevey started to work, he began to draw and sketch with coke chuck in every space he could find. This was proof that Stevey had a very substantial talent to draw and sketch. Stevey's ambition was always to become an artist, however, with his lack of education in grammar school left his ambition by the wayside. And with the attitude of his parents blocking off his rays of hope inside his wishing heart, he still hoped and dreamed that he would accomplish his desire. Stevey dreamed that he soon would make enough money to take a course by mail, and later on through a special art education. If he would make good with the course, then he would be off to a bigger city and would enter night school and he would reach his ambition.

Stevey always believed and dreamed that if a person hoped and wished hard enough, his hopes and wishes must become true one day. He would enter art school in the big city. What a sweet dream and firm determination, if only it could be accomplished.

One day at work as Stevey freshly reviewed his dreaming mind, the time was nearing when he will leave the filthy smokey coke yard, and soon he would look into a new and better future. Yes, the coming fall he would leave the coke yard and would venture to places where he would accomplish his desire to complete his art education. And finally, he would become a famous artist.

Stevey Nagy was emerged in his deep thoughts in a particular moment hardly knew what he was doing. For his thoughts roamed somewhere far into the unknown world. While Stevey was in deep thought, he reached a huge pile of dumped ashes. He backed the horse with a loaded cart of ashes to the edge of the dumping pile. While he was sitting on the front of the cart, the horse backed too far to the edge and the loaded cart over balanced itself and quickly dragged the cart, the horse and Stevey down a huge pile of ashes several hundred feet long. They began to roll over several times before they reached the bottom. Stevey Nagy survived with a broken back and several ribs were also badly crushed. The animals two front legs were broken and was relieved from its misery and agony with a bullet to the head.

Stevey was a human being who would like to be relieved of his misery and agony, but perhaps that was his destiny.

Stevey Nagy never became an artist. He spent several years in the hospital and when he finally recuperated and returned home, other complications from his youth began to take effect and Stevey never did recover.

Early ventures in his mere childhood in the coke yards, greediness for more money by his parents, insufficient rest and sleep during his early school days, a disease had set into his young and tender body long before he had back broken. Possibly he would have a chance for complete recovery, or at least live, if he had not been physically destroyed in his early age. Tuberculosis had developed and Stevey Nagy became the victim of greediness for money. At the age of twenty-two, Stevey Nagy died, perhaps of a broken heart, but yet he died with a smile on his lips, perhaps glad that the death relieved him of further misery and bitter agony from this world.

Stevey's sacrifices were not in vain. Many teachers and educators of that region began to sigh, for they saw the greatest danger in such practices as some of the foreigners brought from their native lands, and successfully integrated these practices into the American way of life. The school heads and prominent educators foresaw a complete ruination of many school children and bean to seek a remedy to correct this situation and save the school children from this plague. District school heads began to get together and firmly resolved with determination sent a delegation to the state legislature to demand law enactment that would prohibit children and women to engage in such work at the coke yards.

Unanimously, every school head, every teacher and every citizen began to fight the evil which began to spread more and more over the entire region.

Stevey's sacrifice saved many other children from similar early death as he had to die. Finally, later on in years, the legislation enacted into law prohibiting school children working in coke yards or coal mines until the age of sixteen.

This was the sad and pitiful fate of a young talented Stevey Nagy. His parents wanted wealth, wanted money, and more money despite having to sacrifice the life of their child.

The Nagys had accumulated several thousand dollars during their stay in the United States. After Stevey's death, they felt humiliated, somewhat responsible for his early death and decided to return back to Hungary. In the late spring in the year 1914, the Nagys left the United States for Hungary. The very day the Nagys stepped on their native soil, a spark ignited a powder keg of the first "World War."

The Nagys were caught in the very beginning of the war. Their country at that time was known as Austria-Hungary which declared war on little Serbia.

After the war was over, news had reached this country about the Nagys. The news dispatched to certain friends of the Nagy family that the entire family had been annihilated by the war. A top price had been paid for their greediness for money and destroying not just one life, but the entire family of the Nagys.

Steve Nagy's body lay in one of the mining town small cemetery where his soul looks down, and perhaps proud that his body lies in the land of the free, the "United States of America."

# XIII

## PREACHER BENNY

Despite his real name being Benjamin Orliss, he was best known all over the entire mining camps as Preacher Benny. Many did not know or did not care to know the real name of Ben Orliss. Evidently, it seemed that Preacher Benny did not mind that people called him by this name. He seemed somewhat delighted and proud if he heard his name called Preacher Benny.

Preacher Benny acquired this name in his forties. When he realized all the worldly enjoyments of adventure, luxuries, money, women, good times and bars and saloons were only temptations to lose the only precious part of a human being that he possessed was his soul. Preacher Benny had realized after many heartaches and hardships and bad luck through his entire young life, that all this world could offer a man or woman was temporary and empty happiness.

The Orliss family were a lifelong farming family in the coal mining area. From the beginning, the Orliss family began to take small acreage for rent or on a crop sharing basis. After a difficult struggle, the Orlisses finally bought a sizable acreage of land in the nearby vast mining area where they succeeded to be foremost among all the areas farmers.

The Orliss children were reared under strict rules in the home with religious and obedient requirements. Eziekel Orliss was a good provider for his family, but also a strict father in raising his family. His children must obey the rules to the point, and his wife shall not interfere at no time when punishment was allotted to his children if punishment was necessary for mischievous acts.

Despite that Benny was reared under strict guidance in his home, he had ideas of his own germinating in his head. He was carefree as well as a free thinker. And finally, he began to think that farm life is not the place for him. Benny wished to see more, to see the country wide open. And littler by little he commenced to plan how to venture into the world.

As Benny reached his fifteenth birthday, he ventured out from the farmhouse, like a little bird when it flew out of the nest for the first time. As the young bird is lured out of its nest by the opposite tree or nearby flower, or other birds that are flying past its nest unaware that there are many misfortunes awaiting it after leaving the nest. Perhaps a cat's eye focused and is impatiently waiting for him, or maybe the rain and wind may overpower the bird, and he may perish in its inexperienced adventure.

Like Benny Orliss, anxious to see the world that offers so much like adventure, excitement, happiness and great opportunity for some. Atop of that, he was lured by others whom he knew from his boyhood and classroom. They began to talk to him about the coal mine and how much money they are making in the pit. This doubly encouraged Ben Orliss.

An opportunity came to Benny when one of his older friends was willing to take Benny to the mine. Despite his father's objection and his mother's plea, Benny went to work in the pit.

Benny was husky and a willing worker and quick learning any trade that came into his hands. He was handy with all kinds of tools from the experience at home repairing farming equipment and building fences and barns.

For about two years Benny stayed in the mine and made particularly good money which he saved. But as Benny grew to manhood, he began to get new ideas about life. He thought that he should see more of the country and not wasting his life in the coal mines. Benny quit the coal mine and ventured farther into the unknown world. Benny moved from state to state just long enough to make some money to keep on moving.

When Benny reached his twenty-first birthday, he crossed more than thirty states. While on his move from state to state, Benny worked many different trades. He worked as a rancher, carpenter, mason, on the railroad, mills, a factory, as a lumberjack, ship-hand, dock worker, a waiter in a hotel and a pipefitter. Many different jobs he tried as he journeyed from state to state.

As soon as Benny would save several hundred dollars, he was on the move to another state. He would not begin to work until he exhausted his entire savings. At that point he would seek a different field of work.

When Benny reached manhood, he became fearless and unconquerable in his ideas. Whenever Benny got into an argument with an individual, or a fist fight, even if he were beaten the first time, he would never give up. He had to fight his enemy until he was victorious if it took months. He never gave up!

During his travels over the states, Benny met different kinds of people. Some good and some extremely bad. He had mixed acquaintances. He learned how to drink and mix with bad company that helped him to spend his money.

It seemed that despite all the adventure, excitement and all the worldly goods, Benny became disgusted, homesick, and decided to return home. In a few months Benny was home again from his adventure seeking and opportunities. After being home several months, Benny met a very refined young lady with deep religious rearing. And after several months of their acquaintance, they got married.

But even through marriage, Benny did not follow his father's footsteps in farming. Benny changed jobs constantly during his first few years of his married life. But Benny was a man that could not stand shouting and abusive language from his bosses. This is the reason he changed jobs often. After changing jobs many times and shooting for every angle in life, upon the advice of his wife, Benny settled back into the coal mine. However, this did not last awfully long. The First World War broke out and Benny was subject for the draft and he was drafted into the American Navy. Fortunate enough, Benny returned unscratched from the war after one year of service. Benny went back to the mine, but meanwhile, he begins to get a new idea in his head. He began raising fighting rooster cocks entering them into fighting contest and accepted gambling on his cocks. In a years' time, Benny had the best pair of fighting cocks in the entire vicinity. Benny won and lost money on the cocks and made no gains, rather is loses mounted up.

Benny's wife thanked God one day when the police came and raided the barn where the fighting was going on. Thus, Benny gave the rooster fighting idea away.

Well, Benny settled back in the mine. As the years passed by, his attitude changed to a more realistic life. As he worked in the mine, he became aware of the hazards the men faced every moment of their life while in the pit. Benny began realizing seriously about his possibility of being killed in a mine accident. He thought that if he were suddenly killed, what would happen to his soul. But something unexpectedly happened. Benny was stricken with a peculiar disease. Benny lies in the hospital for four months like a piece of trash. He could not move using his own strength. In those four months, Benny Orliss, alias Preacher Benny, meditated and meditated. He concluded and realization that the worlds promise of adventure, happiness and lures to the gay and laughing crowds is all worthless and empty.

As Benny lie on his hospital bed, a dim light came on which denotes that it is silent time, timer to sleep. But Benny could not rest. Benny was preparing his mind for something greater than rest. Benny clinched his hand tightly, closed his eyes and whispered, "O Lord, you have been kind and good to me all my life. You have granted me many graces, but I abused them. I disgraced your divinity, O Lord, forgive me and give me one more opportunity to serve you. I promise you O Lord, I will serve you with all my might. Please O Lord?"

With this solemn prayer, Benny dozed out into a sound sleep. One week later, Benny left the hospital and began to fulfil his promises.

One day while Benny was sitting in his chair still recuperating, he spoke to his wife. "Mother." Ever since their first baby was born, Benny addressed his wife as mother. He continued, "I made up my mind to return to the Lord." Benny's wife stared with a doubtful expression on her face. But she saw his face very contented and happy and she believed what he said. "Oh Benny! O God, thank you! O Lord, give him the grace that he shall return to you." A joyful tear rolled down his wife's cheek.

For ten weeks Benny Orliss prayed every day on his knees to God to grant his graces and to give him wisdom, to understand the Holy Bible that he can spread the word of God among those that still are lost in the emptiness of the world.

After ten weeks of praying and asking God for his forgiveness and to help him become a Sower of the Gospel, his prayers were answered and abundantly granted. Now Benny Orliss became Preacher Benny.

Benny remained working in the mine where I had the opportunity to meet him. I thanked God that I had this opportunity to meet Benny who showed me the real way to God. Benny was fearless and true and his services were always free wherever he preached. Benny never accepted compensation for his services.

Preacher Benny was well liked among all classes, young and old, Catholics and non-Catholics, Jews, and even pagans or non-believers. He became interested in Sunday school and organized three churches of the Nazarene in which made his life more interesting. Preacher Benny is really a true friend of the human being. But preacher Benny did not like those who tried to make a commercial business out of religion.

This is Preacher Benny. A man who had every opportunity that the world offered, but finally he concluded that all these worldly goods is only temporary and blank without a Godly future.

After travelling to almost every state and having every opportunity for worldly happiness, he concluded that God should be first from whom we shall get the best and everlasting happiness.

When I was writing this chapter, I met Preacher Benny. I asked him, "how he feels and how is everything?" He said, "friend, I feel good as ever, I am happy and content as long as the Lord leaves me here on earth, but I'm ready every moment if the Lord sends for me."

I wish all can say that. Preacher Benny is the best Bible preacher in this vicinity where I live. He understands the Bible where others have doubt. He is an ardent student of the Bible.

Preacher benny is not a three or four hundred dollars a month preacher as long as he remained working in the mine or another industry where he can earn a living with his two good hands. As long as he is able to work, he will refuse to accept any compensation for preaching in the church. Besides, his support to the other various churches is very generous which is a fulfillment of a requirement of the Bible of his ten percent.

I asked Preacher Benny how he can understand the Bible so deeply and had no formal education in Bible studies? His answer was, "that any man who got faith in God, and gave up all the evils of the world, he can and will understand the Bible." He continued, "that every person has enough will power to go right or wrong."

Preacher Benny brought thousands to God. And he continued to spread the word of God wherever he walked. Some just laughed off Preacher Benny, but his work goes on as long as he is able to do so.

Beside his preaching, Preacher Benny is just like many thousands, just a dust eater, just a human worm.

# XIV

## THE MIRANOFFS

Ivan Miranoff, young and husky, broad shoulders and heavily built, a man about thirty. His rugged face was fully covered with hair, an old style and incredibly old Russian custom. His fully grown beard ran down past his chin and down his chest about six or more inches and as well as outwardly. The hair on his face and beard was kind of a reddish-brown.

The Miranoffs immigrated from Russia about a year ago, and with Ivan, he brought seven children. However, the Miranoffs were only married eight years, nevertheless, it seemed somewhat peculiar that they already had seven children in eight years of married life. Well, this can be easily accounted. Two sets of twins were born to the family during these eight years, thus, this helped the Miranoffs to enlarge their family so early, so rapidly.

Ivan was known to the entire miming population as Katzab. It was a popular old nickname for bearded Russians. The children of the camp had lots of fun when they saw Ivan passing in the street. The kids gathered around him and everyone wanted to touch his mystery, the beard. Ivan would stoop down on his knees and let every kid touch his whiskers. The kids got a great kick out of touching his beard.

Ivan also worked in the mine. Young and strong, Ivan never felt tired after a long day's work in the pit. It seemed that the hard work in the pit was just a toy for Ivan Miranoff.

The Miranoffs came from a part of Russia where people were mostly engaged in agriculture. Ivan's wife, Kata was raised and worked all their life on farms before they arrived in this country, the United States of America. Many times, they thought that they would be happier and content in America, they dreamed if they could have enough money to buy a small parcel of ground big enough to keep a cow and a few pigs, a handful of chickens, raise some potatoes, a few heads of cabbage and things that are needed in the kitchen, their dreams would be secure.

Those were Ivan's and Kata's wishes, dreams and desires. One day Kata spoke to Ivan that they should make every effort to save some money and buy a small plot of ground somewhere close to the mine. Kata also suggested that the children could help on the land and around the home. She further suggested that he can work in the mine while he was young, and when age creeps up on him, he can retire and work his piece of land, his little farm. And if something unexpected happened, they could depend on their plot.

Seven children and another expected any day gave kata great responsibility and problems to undertake such a burden as to keep a budget balanced. She had made up her mind that she will save a few dollars of every pay for the proposed little farm.

In those good old days, there were no restrictions in the mining camps to keep cows, pigs or chickens. There also was no restrictions or regulations pertaining to sanitary or stocks, or from where or to whom a person can sell goods. There weas no law enacted concerning stock disease or sanitary laws regarding the selling of milk. Kata had her own plans and dreams. She always thought that families like hers require lots of milk, eggs, butter and meat. Kata began to think more often how to help herself in the kitchen. Oner day she spoke to Ivan, "Ivan, I want you to buy a cow. Just look how much money we can save on milk alone. If we have a cow of our own, we can supply our needs of milk, and still, we could sell some milk to others." Ivan stared at Kata for a while. By Kata's daring suggestion, he grinningly said, "Don't you think that a cow too need feed and care? Did you ever stop to think how much a cow could cost us? And the upkeep of the cow." "Yes, I did, I have been planning this for a long time. I am convinced that the cow will pay for itself in six months. You watch and see." Concluded Kata.

Ivan did not further dispute Kata's argument. He began to think to himself a cow would be a great help to their household. However, he also knew that there is a great deal of work around a cow; to feed her, milk her, to clean the stable daily and many other routine daily chores. He had considered every angle, but he kept mum about the purchasing of a cow.

To Ivan's surprise, a month later, Kata had her cow. The cow provided enough milk for the entire family, and still Kata was able to sell milk in the neighborhood to almost pay for the cow's upkeep.

Kata was a hustling woman. While others were sitting on front porches or in a front room or leaning across the fences gossiping, Kata went around the camp greens and gathered up grass for the cow. What she cannot use, she dried the grass turning into hay and stored it for the winter months which led to less hay to buy for the cow during the winter.

Two months later, Kata bought twenty-five chickens and a pair of small pigs from the money she had saved from selling the milk. The money she used to pay to buy milk was put away to savings for the much-dreamed little farm.

As the time rolls by day by day, month by month, the Miranoffs family increased to eleven members. The oldest boy, Sammy, was fourteen and a very clever young lad with an inventive mind. Sammy could outright imagine and construct a bridge in his mind. He always engaged in assembling bridges, railroads by using small pieces of wood. Ivan and kata often discussed his creative and instructive imagination. They often dreamed, wished and hoped that they could give Sammy schooling to achieve his ambitions. They would like to if things go right to send Sammy to some engineering school, if possible, in the near future.

Also, there were the one set of twin sisters. An exceptionally talented duet tap dancers. With proper training by a dance teacher, the twins could have a very bright future.

The Miranoffs of course, hoped and dreamed and wished in their hearts for the time shall come when they could afford to fulfill their children's wishes, to obtain their ambitions.

A few more months, not even a year, they will send Sammy to an engineering school and the twin sisters will go to dancing lessons in a nearby town. Yes, the time is nearing, it is near, awfully close.

When the time finally arrived, the Miranoffs were ready to send Sammy to an engineering school. Kata had saved several hundred dollars from her only selling of milk. With her hard work, Kata added week by week the desired funds to her savings. She counted the money often. Why not? It was hers, her hard-earned money. She had the right to count the money so her wishes were to be more substantial, more positive.

Kata saved several thousand dollars from her work. With Ivan's savings together, they had about four thousand dollars. However, Kata thought that her savings was not sure and dependable. She always thought that something unexpected could happen then one would have to reach into her savings instead of Ivan's. Despite her fears, her saving fund was increasing week by week.

The Miranoffs dream almost reached reality, but something sudden and unexpected had happened. Ivan was struck by a piece of a foreign object in the eye in the mine. As a result, Ivan completely lost the sight in his eye. He lost several months of work minus one eye.

With Ivan's accident, Kata savings suffered greatly. While Ivan lay in the hospital, she had to reach into her savings to provide for her large family as there was no pay envelope coming to the home for several months.

How grateful Kata was now that she had a cow, some chickens and the pigs. These were her sources on which she solely depended to keep the table full.

While Ivan was in the hospital, time began to work against Kata's savings and they were shrinking considerably. However, another surprise arrived when Ivan was ready to go back to work. The mines began to slacken and work was only available two or three days a week. Under these circumstances, the dreams and planning for Sammy's school was postponed, at least for the time being. The plans and dreams at the Miranoffs for their children's future was uncertain at this time. No one knew how long the mines will slacken.

As time drags on, working conditions did not improve much for a long time. The working conditions lasted for almost a year before things started to pick up.

Ivan's handicap prevented him from making money as he previously did before he lost his eye. As time went by and to keep the family's burden easier, Ivan got a job for Sammy in the pit.

Kata struggled as hard as ever to save her money, her fund. She acquired another cow to gain her lost savings. However, this added more strain on her, but she did not mind. She would never admit that this was hard and strenuous work on her. The continuous work began to undermine her good health. She began to feel tiredness quite often.

Finally, the mines began improving on a normal work schedule. Work began in full force and again, there was plenty of work all over the mining region. The Miranoffs began to pull themselves out of the rut. New hopes alighted again in their hearts. Yes, Sammy will be going to school in the coming fall as they had originally planned. Sammy finally got the opportunity to become an engineer, a bridge constructor, a railroad builder, a great man in the future.

But alas! No one had ever suspected that another blow, a blow more disastrous than the first one had closed in on the Miranoffs household. Ivan's other eye became infected from the wounds of the lost eye. Despite the doctor's efforts to save Ivan's eye, it failed and fear set in that Ivan would lose his other eye.

Ivan Miranoff at the age of forty-five years, became a totally blind man. The small compensation that Ivan received for his eye and kata's remaining savings provided a small plot of land and a small four room house where the eleven-member family settled down for the rest of their lives.

It was rather impossible and unthinkable to send Sammy to school, or the twin sisters lessons for tap dancing. Sammy remained working in the pit to help his mother with the other children, to keep the Miranoff family together. Sammy Miranoff never did get the opportunity to achieve his ambition and remained in the mining pits. The twin sisters never became tap dancers. They remained with their parents and accepted work in the camp. What work! Washing clothes, cleaning houses, the hardest work one could find in the camp. Perhaps they got married after they matured in the mist of the mining camp with buried talent and ambitions.

Whether Sammy achieved his ambition later is unknown. When I last saw him, he was still working in the mine, disgusted, disheartened for his destiny was just to be just a dust eater, just another among thousands, a human worm....

# XV

## THE KELLARS

In 1895, Leonard Kellar, a young man of twenty-four, just had been discharged from three years of compulsory service in the army. Carefree and happy, but there was something that dispirited Leo's happiness, no work and not a very bright outlook for his future. Leo had no plans, no blueprint that he could follow for his future. Leo disrobed his uniform but had no place to go, no work, no home of his own when he arrived from the army.

Leo Kellar just matured to manhood and began thinking of his future. What to do? Where to find work? This was the problem of many thousands of Slovakia's young men after being discharged from the army. After these men were discharged from three years of compulsory military service, the government had no concern about their future.

Leo was one of the less fortunate young men because his family did not possess worldly wealth. He was the son of poor parents whose only wealth were two good healthy hands on which they depended on to make their earthly living. Once in a while, a few letters would arrive to some families from their loved ones who not long ago immigrated to America. In those letters to wives, parents or relatives, Leo learned that the men were doing very well in America. This proved to Leo that they must be doing well because they would send money back to their families very often. This incited Leo to think more about leaving for the new world.

Leo finally decided to give the new world a chance, the new country called the United States of America. Leo obtained an address from one of his friends who worked in a coal mine somewhere in Pennsylvania. Yes, but hoa! There was Anna, his girl, his faithful sweetheart. She patiently waited for him for three long years while he was in the army. He just cannot leave her here and walk away from her. He would break her heart. He needs to talk to her before he made his final decision. They together must plan for their future. He must see her and talk to her first. A few days later, Leo disclosed his plans, his final decision to Anna which brought her to tears and great grief. Anna, sobbing profusely said, "Oh Leo, you have no heart. You deceived me, Leo." Anna weeps silently as Leo stood there watching Anna cry. Leo was now in despair; he did not want to hear or see Anna cry. "Do not be alarmed my dear. I do not mean to leave you here forever; I did not mean to deceive you darling." Leo took her into his arms and held her close to him. He then again to whisper to her, "Anna dear, I want to tell you of my plans, of my decision. It is for our future Anna darling, for you and me." Leo paused for a moment, just for a moment than pressed a kiss on Anna's lips which were trembling. Then he continued, "you see Anna, here in our native home, we have no future. I cannot find work here and we have no home of our own, and there is no bright and promising outlook for our life together. Leo paused again. Both meditated for a while. Anna also realized that Leo was right. But the fear, the fear that When Leo left her, he would soon forget her and she would just remain waiting, waiting forever.

Another short pause and Leo whispered into Anna's ear, "you see Anna, we can get married now, then I will go to America and then as soon as I can make enough money, I will send for you Anna. You see, I have to borrow the money for my trip. Who would lend us money for both of us to travel to America." Anna was already aware that they have no friends who would trust them and lend them money for both to travel to the new world. The only security was Anna being left behind until Leo paid his debt for his trip, then he could send for Anna.

A little happy wedding occurred a few days after. Then after a few happy days of married life, Leo departed his lovely wife to the unknown and strange world they called America.

Two months later, Leo found himself in the darkness in a Pennsylvania coal mine. Those were trying days for Leo. Anna was on his mind constantly as he worried every minute what she was doing, whether she had a home, something to eat, was she still crying, or whether his parents are kind to her. His thoughts roamed constantly in his head.

Day by day Leo counted the dollars and cents that he has earned in the mine. Every day he counted how much more he needed to pay for his trip, to pay for Anna's trip. Daily, Leo walked to the post office to see if he received a letter from Anna.

It was about a year since Leo arrived in the United States. And at this point, he had saved enough money to send for Anna. At the same time, Leo received a letter from Anna saying that a baby boy was born to them who was named after both grandfathers, Johnny.

Let us visit the Kellars ten years later after Anna had arrived in America, after the Kellars had settled in one of the mining camps in Pennsylvania.

Johnny is ten years old now and a class leader in his school room. Mickey was eight, Leo Jr. is six Anna four and little Mary was two. Three boys and two girls and a stork started circling over the Kellar's house.

Leo was a good worker and provider for his family. He loved his wife and children. Leo Kellar never loafed in a saloon or pool room as many other men did. He was strictly a home body. He always stayed with his family. The Kellars decided that America will be their future home, they were proud that they have the opportunity to become American by naturalization through one of the American courts. All they had from little Slovakia were sad and bitter memories. They felt no reason to return to their native land. For they saw a more abundant and opportune future, more free and happier living in America.

The Kellars have their dreams and plans also. They dreamed and planned for the betterment for their children. They wanted to give to their children everything that America offered. Education and equal opportunity for all. They saw brightness in their children which gave them encouragement for their dreams and plans.

The Kellars began sensing and realizing that there are more and better opportunities for advancement for their children's future in the larger cities than around the coal mining camps. They foresaw that children in cities have better chances for a better education and advancement in choosing their vocations for a future life.

The Kellars have friends here and there. Some in various cities scattered across America. They began corresponding with their friends in many different cities. In one of their letters, they brought up the subject that they would consider moving to the city. The Kellars think that if things in the city are better for their children, than they must decide for the greatest opportunity for the family.

In replies from their letters, an encouragement came from many of their city friends advising them that city life and work are more advantageous for people who have children. Some of their friends even revealed their standings with property and valuables. This kind of news from their friends doubled the Kellar's desire to move to some city and try new surroundings, a new field of living in this new country. The Kellars were deciding for better or worse. But the Kellars carefully weighed and considered before making a final decision. They had looked at every angle of different circumstances around the mines as well as the city.

It was early in the fall when the Kellars made their decision that they will try the city. One day Leo made a remark to Anna saying, "Well, Anna, I will finish this year in the mine. I will work until Christmas. We can visit our friends during the holidays and I can try out this city work." Leo paused and then glanced at Anna which seemed that she did not approve of Leo's ideas. But Leo continued, "while in the city, I can try out the work in a few places and I can look around and find all about the city, whether we shall move or not. You know, I still can come back to the pit if we find out the city is not the way we expected." Leo pauses and aimlessly looked at the floor. "I do not think we all should go. It would be best that you go alone and try out the work. Find out the condition, and also whether or not there are opportunities that are better for all of us, especially our children. Then if it is in our favor, you can lease a home while you are there." Anna spoke those words from her rocking chair where she was sitting holding two-month-old Vilma in her arms. She again continued, "we cannot tell what kind of weather we may have for the holidays and travelling with six small children is not much fun."

Oh, what a beautiful dream! Carefully chosen plans. What a sincere and far-reaching concern for the welfare and future of their children.

However, it is natural. A human being is the most perfect creation in the whole world, always dreaming, always planning for its future betterment, to achieve its dreams, its aims and desires. It is true, some did, some will, some try, some would achieve their objects, but many, many just dream, plan, wish, and many will and were disrupted in the mid of their sweet dreams and wishes.

If the Kellars in the mist of their dreams and plans could foresee just thirty days ahead of their life, they would be stricken with horror and despair.

It is best for the human being that God's secret for his or her destiny are hidden and unknown. For many human beings would end their lives from horror and fear, which unknowingly creeps slowly toward a person. Which is their destiny.

The Kellars wholeheartedly agreed that they will celebrate the coming Christmas, exceptionally different. Yes, they will celebrate the coming Christmas because the next Christmas they would not be living in the mining camp because they will have moved to the city.

They will miss all their friends that they have acquired during their stay at the mining camp. And perhaps there will be a different circumstance in their home the next Christmas.

The beginning of next December Anna began buying things for the nearing holidays, for the coming Christmas. The most joyous, most happy holidays of the entire year. The children started to count the days. St. Nick, then St. Lucy, Christmas was at the threshold. Two more weeks, one more week and then Christmas.

Anna was restless the whole night. In the morning when she arose from bed, she felt oddly for some unknown reason, fear in her heart. She packed Leo's lunch bucket as usual, as she did every morning when she got up. As she touched the bucket, she shivered, why? She did not know. Anna stood motionless for a while. She had her hands stretched out for Leo, as he kissed her goodbye. She walked speechless toward the door behind Leo as he disappeared into the darkness of the night.

Anna outstretched her hands again, as to call Leo back, but he was gone. She stops! "What is the matter with me?" She thought to herself as she closed the door. "It is the strain from last night" Anna whispered to herself, and her fearful tension lessened.

The baby's cry interrupted her from the strange and fearful thoughts as she walked toward the crib and took the baby with her to bed.

The day was sad and gloomy. Darkness of the low clouds hanging over the mining camp seemed that they would fall to earth at any moment. The mist dragged slowly and low making it more miserable.

It was about nine o'clock in the morning and Anna still in a fearful mood stood by the window, just staring. Then suddenly she heard a terrific roar. The house seemed to move as the whole camp shuttered as an earthquake had happened. Anna could not move for a moment. Then a whistle on the mine tipple began to shrill as for a fire. The sound of the whistle seemed sad, so terrifying for some reason, or it appeared to Anna the way the whistle shrilled. A crowd began to rush and gather around the mine, men, women and children all ran toward the mine. "What happened?" Someone cried out from the gathering crowd. "Explosion in the mine?" was the answer!

It was a very pitiful scene. No person could really describe the sadful expressions on the hundreds of men, women and children's faces who had gathered around the ***pitmouth***.

Screaming of women and children, the terrifying shrill of the whistle pictured a heartbreaking scene. Men moaned, children screamed, wives and mothers sending hysterical cries towards the dark clouds.

Some in their night clothes, some bare footed with their eyes turned staring blindly to the mouth of the mine from which a nasty odor of smoke rolled out in heavy clouds where 320 miners, burned, perhaps suffocated or possibly killed by the terrific force of the explosion.

Many wives and mothers fainted at the scene and dropped and fell on the cold and muddy mine grounds. Some wished that their lives would end where their sons and husbands died. Many will have horrific problems in their future from the result of the mine explosion.

A tent was erected not far from the mine where charred bodies of the miners were laid before final burial. Among these 320 miners, one was Leo Kellar. The faces of the miners were burnt and swollen beyond recognition.

Their entire bodies and faces were unidentifiable. The wives and mothers could only recognize their loved ones if they had some identifying object on them, or by their clothes if they had any clothes remaining on their bodies.

What a contrast! Just a short thirty days ago, Leo Kellar with his wife Anna, looked forward to the future with the sweetest dreams and plans for them and their children's future.

Just a few weeks ago the Kellars were determined to change their location. Too abandon the mines and look for a new location in the city where their children could receive the best America has to offer. A better education, more opportunities for advancement, for the future lives of their children. Oh, sweet dreams and plans.

Leo Kellar died in the horrible explosion with the sweet dreams and plans on his mind when the horrible flames with a terrific force knocked him down to his death. Perhaps his last thought was about Anna and his six ambitious children.

Imagine the shock Anna had to go through. It took years for Anna to recover. Whether her dreams and plans were ever fulfilled is unknown. The circumstances Anna faced with her six children denied her to make any decision to move on for a long time.

Johnny, the oldest boy was forced to the pit at an early age to help support the family. He was the only provider. He had to take his father's place to provide for the family needs.

A year or so later, Mickey followed Johnny to the pit to also help support the family. These first few years after the explosion were trying years for Anna Kellar.

After Johnny and Mickey began to start work in the mine, their plans to move to the city were abandoned, at least for the time being.

Years later I heard that Johnny got married and settled permanently in the mining camp. Mickey also remained in the mine to support the family.

Another family's dreams and plans were just, "dreams and plans."

# XVI

## THE GIBSONS

Gilmore Gibson, with his wife and four small children immigrated to the United States from England. But he did not come on the famous Mayflower, but on a less famous ship in 1901. It was to his advantage because he would not have to convince anyone or dispute that he came on the Mayflower.

Gil worked as a coal miner in England, but when he heard that the mining industry was developing to a great extent in the United States, he decided to immigrate with his family to America.

Working conditions in the mining industry in England was not steady and not much promise at this time. He thought that if he would not find better conditions in the United States, he would not lose much except travelling expenses which cost about two-hundred dollars. Curiosity more than anything else lured Gibson to the United States of America. Being a coal miner in England, Gibson decided to remain with the same job here, a coal miner, for he had no other trade to follow.

The Gibsons have a huge advantage over the other immigrants from other parts of Europe, they could speak the English language, while others had learned to speak, which for some was quite difficult.

The Gibsons had three boys and a girl. Chrissy eight, Lennie six, Dickey three- and one-year old Nancy. The Gibsons settled in the mining camp with the other colorful mixture of foreigners.

The coal mining industry in England was not much further ahead education wise than the people from East and Central Europe. Many of the coal miners in England were illiterate. Some could read printed words, but most could not read or write at all. At that time, the mining industry in England consisted of the lowest class of people in the entire empire of England. Gil Gibson did not have much education himself, in fact, Gil did not care much about education until he arrived in the United States. When Gil arrived in this country, he began to be interested in newspapers and magazine readings. He later on, he would pick up a book occasionally. This helped him quite a bit. And the more he read the more he liked to read. Gil learned more in the states in a short time then he did in his entire life in England.

As a man with knowledge of the English language, he had more and better opportunities for advancement in the mine. In those days when the coal mines began to spread all over the region, and more and more mines every year, a need for supervisory help was felt all over the mining industry. Every mine felt the shortage of supervisory help.

To become a supervisor, better known as a foreman or a fire boss, one must possess a certificate. To qualify for a certificate, the miner must appear before a board of examiners for a test of knowledge of mining laws and familiarities as to general mining.; different gases and their dangers. Also, he must have a certain time completed of experience in the mine. If successfully one would pass the written examination, an oral examination was given which was a formality. If successfully passed, a certificate was awarded to the miner by the Department of Mines.

Despite Gil's poor writing and reading skills, Gibson took the exam and passed the test for a fire boss certificate. Immediately after he obtained the certificate, he was hired as a fire boss in the mine. A fire boss in the mine is a man who makes the examination of the pit before any man can enter the mine. He has to ascertain whether the mine is free of any danger of gasses or any other consisting hazards. A job that yields more money than any other ordinary mine work, and the work is much easier than that of a miner.

Well, the Gibsons did not discover anything unusual in their children, until oner day, when their cooking stove blew up into pieces. It was Chris, experimenting with chemistry. Chris was always interested and engaged in mixing liquids, always finding something new to mix. One day Chris gathered all kinds of small bottles from the medicine cabinet and began experimenting, mixing, heating, cooking and boiling until the mixture ignited and exploded ripping the cooking stove into small fragments.

Chris experiments was too expensive for the Gibsons. They had to buy a new stove; however, Chris's parents did not punish him for his ideas and searching experiment. Nevertheless, Chris was lucky enough to escape serious injury.

Despite the explosion of his mixtures, it does not scare him from further research and experimenting. It was his hobby, chemistry. With Chris experimenting, and the explosion of the mixtures gave the Gibsons an idea. A dream that Chris should be given every opportunity to become a chemist. Yes, the Gibsons made up their mind to dream and plan for the three other children's ambitions and try to discover their talent. They decided that as soon as Chris finishes grade school, which was one more year, they would move to one of the larger cities for the sake of their children's ambitions and talents, which they began to display during their grade school. Yes, they will leave the coal mining region and will settle in one of the big cities, where more opportunity was waiting for his children and their talents and ambitions.

That was the daily dreams and plan, their wishes, just like many other thousands of miners and their families. The Gibsons wanted to see that their family got the best that America offers to millions who seek opportunities for their future life. The Gibsons thought by staying around coal mines, their children would never have an equal opportunity as those in larger cities. In anyone of the large cities, youngsters can attend night trade school or other educational institutions. But living in the coal mining region, in the country, there are no such opportunities.

Under this impression, the Gibsons firmly resolved and decided to migrate to a larger city in the United States. While Chris was still in grade school, they will find out through their friends from the city, which city would be the best suitable for them.

Lennie too, also had a talent. He could draw or sketch almost any kind of object. He could glance at a person and sketch he or she very quickly without any hardship. Lennie displayed a skillful talent at the age of twelve. Chris and Lennie's talents encouraged the Gibsons to make their final decision to move to the big city.

The Gibsons had saved several hundred dollars for which they would buy a home in the city to avoid the high rental costs.

It was the beginning of summer when the Gibsons decided that they will move to the city before the winter sets in. Gil was to give his employer two weeks' notice that he intended to terminate his employment and receive his full pay. At the end of the two weeks, he would not have to wait any longer for a full pay envelope.

In the middle of their sweet dreams and plans, something serious happened and disrupted their ideal plans and dreams. Diana, Gil's wife, after a pause of five years of being childless was expecting a new baby. The Gibsons had planned that the time they would move to the city, the baby would be three months old. However, difficulty had arisen with the birth of the baby. Diana had to be taken to the hospital immediately upon the doctor's advice. But despite all efforts of the best doctors, Diana lost her life along with the baby. This sad tragedy upset the Gibson's plans and dreams entirely. Gil had to hire a housekeeper to keep the home in order while the children were at school and he was at work. Nancy was just a little over six years old and just began school and was too small to be taking care of the home.

The savings which the Gibsons accumulated for the new home in the city began to vanish quickly. The plans and dreams which the Gibsons thought about for years had been shattered in a few short weeks. There were no bright outlooks for the Gibson's future.

Chris, still ambitious, still full of dreams and hopes to become a chemist grew more dim by the day. Chris gave up his desire for the time being. With hope that someday an opportunity may come and his dreams will come true. Mixing chemicals would become a reality to him some day. With these hopes in the back of Chris's mind, he obtained a job in the mine pit with the intention to make some money so he could enter a chemistry school and achieve his dreams, his ambition.

Several years past since Diana's death. The Gibsons slowly overcame their sadness and grief over the wife and mother. Nancy was now able to help around the house, and upon her suggestion, they let the housekeeper go. It would reduce their household expenses, which began to exceed their income. Nancy knew and was aware that keeping house is very responsible hard work. But she sacrificed her future to keep the family harmonious and intact.

Lennie also got a job in the mine and the Gibsons began to get back on their feet. They started to put a few dollars away. They began to think despite mother no longer being around, about their abandoned plans and dreams anew.

It was not too late yet. They still can move to the city and begin a new life as they originally planned years ago. No, it is not late yet.

While the deep sorrow and grief was barely healed at the Gibson home, they began thinking of restoring their past dreams and plans, and another handicap began to settle at the Gibson's house.

Gil Gibson started to cough steadily. It seemed that a cold had settled in his chest. Despite taking many different types of cold and cough medicines, the cold lie in his chest constantly. His breathing became heavier weekly. Nights became restless for him. He hardly could sleep a few hours during the night. He hoped that the terrible cold would relieve him since had taken every kind of known medicine.

The breathing got heavier instead of being relieved. It appeared that his cold went from bad to worse. Finally, Nancy summoned the doctor to give him a thorough examination. After the doctor examined Gil, he found that Gil did not have a cold, but discovered he had miner's asthma.

The doctor advised Gil to quit the mine at once if he wanted to be rid of this dreadful plague. The only way to obtain relief the doctor advised, "was to quit working in the mine to avoid the coal dust."

Quit the mine? Where can he go? If Diana had not died, they would be living in the city now. He could have had a better job somewhere in a mill or factory. The children would have a better chance to reach their ambitions. They could have achieved for what they desired.

But now! Where can he go? No money, no health, no work! Who would hire him now? Yes, I am done, I am through! This was Gil's thoughts. Gil Gibson can work no longer. The plague, the miner's asthma tortured him day and night. His condition did not improve but began to worsen daily.

Chris and Lennie gave up their hopes with regret. They realized that their father is unable to work anymore. They could not leave him now. They could not leave him homeless without any support. They decided to sacrifice their own dreams and ambitions which they had long planned.

Later Chris got married and settled in the mining camp. Lennie and Nancy remained home to take care of their father, to give him comfort and love for the few remaining days on this earth.

Nancy also had the opportunity to get married, but she declined with an answer that she would never get married while her father is living. Lennie still hoped some day after his father's death, he still could enter some art school. Lennie saved every extra dollar he could in the event that he would have the chance to attend an art school.

Lennie was a rope rider in the mine. A job where he had to ride at the end of a trip of about thirty pit cars up a steep grade to the cars final destination.

It was in November, about a year after Chris got married. A rope on a loaded trip broke at the peak of the grade. The loaded cars roared back the grade and finally crashed and beneath the wreckage, Lennie's body was found, cold and dead. The shock was so great to Gil Gibson, that when he heard of the tragedy, he dropped dead.

Father and son were buried the same day and lay opposite of wife and mother in a little cemetery in one of the mining camps. Rev. Karin, Father Daniel and Preacher Ben, Dr. Graymore were there to pay last tribute to father and son, a tribute to the men who went to the mine day in and day out throughout their lives, as human worms.

Sweet dreams and plans. After many years of beautiful dreams, all was there in the little cemetery, perhaps, still their dreams, but a dream of a different world, a world which is unknown to human beings.

Three little tombstones sit close together, where once a year Chris and Nancy, with tears in their eyes visit the sacred place. They place a wreath on the tombs of, father, mother, and brother.

# XVII

## MODERN MAGI

Three young men sitting around a small business table, in a small ordinary office, a doctor's office in a mining camp.

The three men were, Dr. Graymore, Rev. Karin and Father Daniel. They were discussing the plans that Rev. Karin and Father Daniel had been considering for weeks. Dr. Graymore heartily approved of their plans and immediately pledged himself to give all his spare time and full support to help promote the plans. Dr. Graymore predicted with great enthusiasm that the idea will and must succeed.

It was the beginning of March, long before any sport activities would start, when these three Magi gathered in Dr. Graymore's office to map out their first activities for the youngsters living in the camp. Rev. Karin had suggested that a baseball club be organized to begin with the activities. Father Daniel frowned his eyebrows for moment weighing Rev. Karin's suggestion. Then he spoke, "I am afraid, Rev. Karin, that a single team or club would not answer our aims. One team would not create enough interest among the boys in the camp."

Father Daniel paused momentarily, and was to continue, but Rev. Karin interrupted him and said, "Why wouldn't it?"

"Well, it may be difficult to organize boys from two different churches into one team. We would not satisfy all. We cannot play the youngsters on one team," Father Daniel said, trying to explain his point of view.

But Rev. Karin again interrupted by asking, "Why? I cannot understand what you mean, Father?" Father Daniel again attempted to raise his point of view and continued.

"Since we cannot play all the youngsters from both churches, some of the youngsters will be disappointed and would start trouble and discourage others not to play, to quit. A friction would develop, and our efforts would be futile," concluded Father Daniel. A silence for the moment prevailed.

Then Dr. Graymore who has been listening all this time spoke up. "That is very true what Father Daniel said." Again, a silence for a few seconds.

Father Daniel then suggested, "You know what, Rev. Karin, you and I can organize a team in our respective churches, then we can work out a season schedule for so many games during the season. This way we would have real competition between the teams."

"Father, you have got something there. It is wonderful. And it will and must work."

"It is a swell idea and I am 100 percent for it," commended Dr. Graymore with great enthusiasm.

"At the end of the season, we can have a playoff of a three or five game series, like the big leagues do. Then we could give a prize to the winning team, and a banquet dinner to the entire membership of both teams."

Father Daniel paused and waited for a moment if the two listeners had anything to add, but they only stared at Father Daniel. Seeing that neither one had anything to say, he then again continued. "This, I think would stir up enough interest among the entire community, young and old alike."

"Great idea Father Daniel, great idea," complimented Rev. Karin on Father Daniel's suggestion.

"Swell idea! Well, since we laid the foundation of the plan, I will donate twenty-five dollars to our future sports fund," Dr. Graymore said as he pulled out his pocketbook from his coat and lay a twenty and a five-dollar bill on the table.

"Just hold on to it, Doctor. You are going to be the treasurer for our club, Pleasant Valley Athletic Club," said Father Daniel as he pulled out his wallet and laid a five-dollar bill on the table, his only possession, saying, "I pledge twenty-five dollars to the club, but I can only pay my pledge in five install-ments." Rev. Karin made a similar pledge, and also laid a five-dollar bill on the table, the only five dollars that he had to live on for the next six days.

The following Sunday, both Father Daniel and Rev. Karin announced to their respective churches of the proposed baseball clubs. Each pastor called a meeting for those interested in the sport.

The youngsters, their fathers, the whole camp who were interested in the sport were invited to attend the first meeting for organizing the baseball teams. The announcement was accepted with great enthusiasm by all, young and old. The meeting was unexpectedly large in both churches. Many lads enrolled to play ball, which assured that the sport will succeed without difficulty. Also, the school personal favored the idea and pledged their full financial support and cooperation.

The two ministers began to breathe easier. Their anxiety lessened after they succeeded in organizing the camp's youngsters into baseball clubs. The public also commented on the brilliant idea, as while as the mining company. They donated money, men and horses, and prepared the baseball field and kept maintenance of the field during the season. This required several men with a team of horses. The following pay day, the mine officials made personal efforts to collect donations at the pay window for support of the two teams.

Dr. Graymore, by the time the practices had started, he had all the goods necessary in his office to play ball, to begin the season.

The youngsters turned out on the field gratefully. The two ministers watched the kids play eagerly. And with great interest, they tried to detect the leader of the gang. However, the ministers saw that the lads had their hearts on playing baseball. No wonder that the three Magi, Father Daniel, Rev. Karin and Dr. Graymore smiled with great satisfaction.

With joy in their hearts, and very hopeful for the future, the three men were finally convinced that they had succeeded, that they began to end the evil among the youngsters who were terrorizing the community. They had finally wiped out this major problem.

However, a shadow of fear, a fearful anticipation still worried Father Dan-iel, day and night. Something told him that trouble was brewing, and that the three men will have to face greater dangers yet.

The three Magi met very often to get everything ready for opening day of the baseball season. They had been going over the schedule which the ministers had announced to the churches. They checked and ascertained whether the schedules are posted all around the community so the entire population of the camp would attend the opening game.

It seemed since the youngsters were engaged in baseball practice, the pranks and mischief around the camp had ceased. There was not one single complaint heard from anyone once the youngsters started to practice baseball on the playing field.

After a few hours of hard practice, the youngsters did not feel much to wonder to go out in the evenings. They stayed at home and rested during the evening hours, so they will be fresh and lively the following day. They were only anxious to play ball.

Finally, the day arrived when the first baseball game was to be played. The people from the camp, the entire community turned out to see their favorite team win their first baseball game. The ministers now became opponents. Each one stood awfully close to his team and talked to the youngsters, like a father tom his own children, The ministers gave their final instruction to each individual player. They called on each player and talked with them with spirited encouragement. They talked to them to be cool and fearless with the ball, and to always be under control. Yes, the fatherly instructions to the young lads, were like a balm on an ached heart.

The youngsters with glitter in their eyes, joy in their hearts, for the first time in their lives, with snappy uniforms on were going to play real baseball. Oh, how happy, how these smiling faces were when they ran out to the field when the umpire called, "play ball."

Dr. Graymore was there also. He was there as an impartial member of the clubs. As usual, he handed out candy to the kiddies, but some already knew his tricks, and flatly refused the castor oiled filled candy. But Dr. Graymore was there because he was the backbone of the club, he was the treasurer. He had the possession of all the club's materials, such as balls, bats, gloves, hats, score books and everything else pertaining to the game. He was also there because there might be an injury in the game and would be ready to serve as doctor.

The crowd violently roared with great joy at every play the lads made, which of course gave more encouragement to the youngsters. Well, each team had its followers, however, it was just all in fun, a real American past rime with no indication of any friction between the population of the community, or the opposing teams. On the field, the ministers being opponents had to stay with their team. But in their hearts, they became unparted and inseparable dear friends.

The ministers were there for one in the same cause, the same reason. For a very dear cause, a cause to save souls from evil. To teach the youngsters what is right and wrong. To bring them back from evil and mischiefs. To prevent and uproot the perilous growing gangsterism. To bring the growing generation back to God and warn them of the consequence of bad company. The two ministers with Doctor Graymore united and agreed to work against these evils with all their effort.

The first game ended in a tie. Every person, young and old, left the field happier and content. Why? No one could explain. A greater friendship had developed among the camp's population.

Obviously, the three great Magi were the happiest men in the community. That night, Father Daniel spent many hours in silent prayer kneeling in front of a crucifix thanking God. This was the beginning, the very beginning for which he prayed ever since he arrived at the community finally was granted by the Lord. His greatest desires, his greatest wishes have become a reality. However, Father Daniel, Rev. Karin and Dr. Graymore never anticipated that new troubles, new worries, new headaches were arising the next day.

A thief had been planning to ruin and destroy the work and hardship that these three great men already accomplished. Could these three men find a clue and catch the thief. Will they apprehend the gang leader before he destroys and ruin what they had established?

The gang leader was in despair. He knew he was beaten if he let his gang remain playing ball. He knew that one of the gang's members will disclose his identity, and he would be the subject of the whole community.

The leader resolved that he would break up the ball teams and bring the gang back under his leadership. Yes, he resolved to go to work the very first night after the first game was played. He himself watched the youngsters play and was convinced that the lads had their hearts into the sport. He must prevent the lads from turning away from the gang and command the youngsters to go back into the alleys, back on the streets at night, to steal, to destroy, to cause as much damage to the community as possible.

# XVIII

## THE GANG LEADER

Several weeks have past at the camp since the baseball activities had begun, and life rolled on without any major incident. The young lads were the happiest boys around the mining camp. They were ecstatic that they had the opportunity to play baseball with a regular schedule. And loved the competition between each other. This gave them great thrills and satisfaction. The lads did not want to be bothered with anything else but playing baseball.

The three benefactors, the modern Magi, Rev Karin, Father Daniel, and Dr. Graymore were also three happy men. The population of the vicinity began to praise these three men for their splendid work in the community for the youngsters and for the entire camp.

But as the sport of baseball swung into its prime, something began to slacken the progress of the game. At every game which was played, someone always started trouble and delayed the game and this resulted in fistfights. The trio of Rev. Karin, Father Daniel, and Dr. Graymore began to suspect that someone deliberately was starting the trouble. The further the season went, there never was a game where an argument didn't start, resulting into a fight.

The three men put their heads together and began to work. Father Daniel said, "Gentlemen, we have got work to do. We've got to set up a trap for the troublemaker. What's more, I think we are going to catch the gang leader."

"You think he's the one starting trouble at every game," assessed Rev. Karin.

"Father Daniel is right. Someone is deliberately provoking the troubles at every game," added Dr. Graymore. "I think in the next few games we will catch the culprit," concluded Rev. Karin.

The work of the gang leader began to be felt. Some of the youngsters who were involved in playing ball regularly began to not show up for the games, with different excuses as headaches, sore feet. And some not even appearing on the playing grounds. The trio was convinced that someone had his hands in the many excuses and alibis from the youngsters.

Yes indeed, there was a lad who was a leader of the gang who dissented with the idea of playing baseball. He began to whisper here and there discouraging the lads and ordering them to quit playing ball and keep away from the ball field.

The majority of the youngsters did not heed his orders and warnings but kept playing ball regularly. So, the leader began creating arguments and delaying the games at every possible opportunity.

The following week, after the trio had set a trap for the culprit, which was the first game of the week, the trio was ready to spring the trap and catch the troublemaker, perhaps the gang leader. The game started as usual with great enthusiasm with that with the exception that a few regular players were missing. However, their places were filled with many extras who were anxious to play ball.

Father Daniel scrutinized the crowd and began to watch every move among the crowd. The trouble always starts about the umpire's decision.

The night before this particular game, someone did break into Dr. Graymore's office and stole half of the clubs goods belonging to Pleasant Valley Athletic Club. Whatever was not taken away, it was destroyed and could never be used again. This caused considerable losses to the club, and of course added expenses, because Dr. Graymore had to buy hurriedly new equipment to replace the stolen and destroyed equipment. If he did not purchase the needed items, they would have had to postpone the games. It just would fit the gang leader's wishes to break up the teams.

The trio was determined to go ahead without delay and catch the leader. Now they were positively sure that the leader's action was very desperate to break up both teams.

In the middle of the game, the usual disturbances started, but Father Daniel was right there, and tried to quiet down a lad, who was starting the trouble. Father Daniel called the young lad to the side from the crowd to talk to him and try to convince him that troublemaking is not an American sport. An argument started between the lad and Father Daniel before Rev. Karin and Dr. Graymore, and a few others arrived to join Father Daniel. Then the lad smacks Father Daniel in the jaw.

Joe "Gip" Erceg was the leader of the gang. He was known all over the community as Gip. Gip was born and raised in the mining camp by foreign parents who immigrated to this particular camp. Gip was a lad about thirteen years old, heavy built and stocky. He would constantly curse and was fearless. Because of his extraordinary build, no one was able to guess his age being less than sixteen years old. He was a real troublemaker at the ball games. Many games had to be postponed or called off due to the darkness, just because Gip prolonged the games with his arguments. Many enthusiastic spectators being disgusted of the arguments began to evade the games. They became tired of the arguments that were happening at every ball game that was played.

Gip Erceg belonged to Father Daniel's church. Father Daniel knew Gip from his constant pranks at the church. Gip had incited two altar boys who had served at Mass, to steal the wine that was being used at Mass. Father Daniel than decided since Gip belonged to his church, he would take Gip under his responsibility. He pledged to Rev. Karin and Dr. Graymore that he will talk to Gip his own way to bring him back to, the civilized world, back to being a decent societal member, back to a Christian life.

Father Daniel, despite the pledge he gave to Rev. Karin and Dr. Graymore that he would take responsibility for Gip, and that he would deal with him alone began to worry about this matter. What if he could not bring Gip back to the road of God? Real humanity.

During the week after the incident on the ball grounds, Father Daniel called Gip to his parish house. Gip fearlessly entered the parish house as if nothing had happened. Father Daniel offered Gip a chair and asked him to sit down. Then he began to speak to Gip very softly and from the heart. He said, "Gip, why do you cause so many troubles at every game? Do you think it is the sportsman's way? We Americans do not like this kind of sport. Why do you do this, Gip?"

"It's none of your business what I do. I can do whatever I want, and whenever I please," retorted Gip.

"Listen, Gip, we want all of our friends to be good Christians. Why don't you help instead of creating troubles?" Father Daniel paused and gazed at Gip's disinterested face. Then he again continued, "We let you play ball regularly if you want, or we can let you coach the team. Would you like to join us, Gip?" Father Daniel pleaded.

"I ain't no sissy, you mind your own business. I am going to break up both of your teams, and that you will never be able to bring them together again, you see. And you and that preacher, and that pill man, can't do nothing about it!" Joe Gip Erceg madly snapped back.

"Think it over, Gip. I called you here for your own good. Gip, remember you have gone too far. When you get yourself into trouble, it will be too late to back out." He spoke softly to Gip as tears filled Father Daniel's eyes.

"Awe, who do you think you are? You think that if you are a priest, you can stick your nose in every place. I will do what I please, see," Gip again snapped.

"You know what is going to happen to you, when you will get going again with your troublemaking ways, you will get caught with your gang and the end will come quickly. Then you know where you will land? Father Daniel paused; it seemed like Father Daniel had nothing more to say. Gip turned toward the door, which meant to Father Daniel, that his talk did not affect Gip at all. Then as Gip grabbed the doorknob, Father Daniel concluded, "Whenever you think that your troublemaking is over, come to me and we will talk again. You may now go, Gip. But please remember what I have told you for your own benefit, your own good."

Joseph "Gip" Erceg slowly walked out the parish house. With his head bowed low, and for the first time in his life, Gip felt shameful. But the evil was stronger than Father Daniel's pleas and advice. The growing temptation dragged Gip further and further into gangsterism, to severe mischief and crime.

A week later, Father Daniel again called Gip to the parish house with a thought that Gip may still break away from his evils. He thought that these weekly talks would bring him to consider giving up his bad habits in his young life.

Father Daniel indirectly hinted to Gip, saying, "Joseph, do you know we have been robbed of all our baseball outfits? I just mentioned this to you because you are well acquainted with every lad in this entire community. Would you know who would or could commit such a crime?"

"Hey, what are you trying to do? Pin something on me? I did not do it. No, I do not know anything about your baseball outfits or your club!" shouted Gip. It was evident that Gip began to feel uneasy. Father Daniel's fatherly words quieted him down a little. Then Father Daniel spoke again.

"Look here, Gip, you can trust me. Gip, if you tell me that you did, no one will ever find out. Except me and you. The police are coming tomorrow to investigate the crime and if they will find out who did it, which I am sure they will, then you will pay for the crime very dearly. Tell me, Gip, did you do it?"

Father Daniel's eyes have rested on Gip. Gip hesitated for a while as his eyes stared toward the floor as Father Daniel waited for his answer. "What is going to happen to me if I admit that I did the robbery?" Gip responded alarmed. "Gip, if you promise me that if you will give up your crazy ideas to be a gang leader, and if you promise me that you will never steal or destroy anything, or not to create mischief around the camp, that you give up the gang and quit being its leader, no one will ever know!" Father Daniel responded kindly as he rose from his chair. He then put his hand on Gip's arm and continued, "I will pay for all the damages that you did to the club, and no one will ever ask any questions about you. And furthermore, I will recall the police from investigating the theft."

Father Daniel sat back down in his chair and gazed at Gip who stood there and hesitated for quite a while before he spoke. "Yes, Father, I did the robbery. I am so sorry, Father Daniel. But if you will conceal the robbery and looting, I promise that I will try my best to stay away from these bad habits. Please, Father Daniel."

Yes, Gip admitted that he planned the robbery for some time. He admitted that he hated all three, Father Daniel, Rev. Karin, and Dr. Graymore because he knew that they were determined to bust up his gang. He wanted revenge against the trio. He thought that if he can destroy their equipment and steal their outfits from Dr. Graymore's office, that they would quit. Yes, Gip related to Father Daniel all his misdoings. The deal was made between the two, Gip and Father Daniel.

However, Father Daniel revealed the robbery to Rev. Karin and Dr. Graymore with the understanding that the robbery would remain a secret until Gip himself admits to the robbery voluntarily. Father Daniel wanted to pay for the damages caused by Gip, but the two flatly refused to accept payment for the goods. They decided that they would equally share the losses.

Gip kept his promise that he made to Father Daniel and began behaving. But Father Daniel was not quite sure that Gip would continue as a good citizen. He feared that sooner or later Gip will be tempted and return to evil once more. He knew that Gip, was too deep in his habits and something must be done to save him.

Father Daniel pounded his mind. He searched and tried to think of some idea to return and retain Gip to a decent American and Christian life. Then he struck on a queer idea. An idea that he was determined to try, to attempt and save Gip Erceg from human destruction and bring him into the fold of a real Christian life, to a real life of humanity.

Many people gamble throughout their life. Some gain, some lose, and some just break even. Others are fortunate enough to acquire wealth by gambling, but most are unfortunate and lose all and become tramps and beggars the rest of their life. But these are only worldly possessions. Gold, silver and other valuable securities. With all the wealth in the world, no person could save his soul if they sinned and never repented.

Father Daniel was sitting in his office and emerged deeply in his thoughts. He was thinking of gambling to save a soul from destruction. Father Daniel was willing to spend every dollar he had as well as his willingness to even borrow money, just to succeed to save Gip from evil. He desperately wanted to keep Gip from drifting further and further from being a menace to society.

Let us leave Father Daniel, Rev. Karin and Dr. Graymore with Gip's problem. Let us leave Father Daniel to decide whether he would gamble his whole life's effort to save Joseph Gip Erceg. Let us take a trip through the entire coal region and return to the mining camp where Rev. Karin, Dr. Graymore, and Father Daniel live. Let us find out in the following chapter how thousands of coal miners spend and invest their hard-earned money.

129

# XIX

## THE FIRST WORLD WAR: PROSPERITY

The First World War began in 1914 and an era of prosperity started soon after the war broke out in Europe. The war ushered the United States into make munitions and other war materials at full production and tempo. Factories, mills and mines began to workday and night. Every plant began to work full force, twenty-four hours a day. Millions of unemployed men and women found work.

Two years later, the United States got involved in the war. The sinking of the Lusitania with many American lives being lost, led our government to declare war on Germany, and the Austro-Hungarian Empire.

The war was on, and prosperity smiled on the entire working masses of our United States of America.

The mining industry also worked very well. Coal was in great demand all over the world. The miners were making good money if they wanted to work. Good wages were paid and money was plentiful.

Many thousands of miners were carefree, careless and very foolish on how they spent their hard-earned money. Since they were making plenty of money, they spent it freely, and wanted more. But true enough, they wanted more money the easy way, if there was a way to get it.

Where there is plenty of money to spend, and foolishly, there are always smart people nearby. To take the money away from the foolish miners. That is what happened in the most prosperous years during and after the first world war, until that disastrous and never forgettable crash in the year 1929.

During these prosperous years, every kind of enterprise, companies, and corporations were organizing like mushrooms after a September rain. Gold mines, silver mines, gas and oil wells, automobiles, and even coal mine stock and shares spread like a fishing net all over the entire coal region. Everyone was anxious to get easy money, to get rich quickly.

Hundreds of speculators had found out that plenty of money could be taken in the coal mining field. The speculators flooded the entire coal mining region, every mining camp they began to set their baits, to grab the miner's hard-earned money.

These fictitious companies and corporations got very busy and with full force began to print gilt-edge shares and certificates, which was the main bait for the miners. These fictitious companies set out their nets throughout the mining camps and began to work on the free spending miners. The heads of these companies hired men and women, preferably good talkers. They gave them two weeks training on how to approach the miners. After the training was completed, they were sent out to the mining camps to begin their scheme. The nets were stretched and the trap was set. These trained agents swarmed the mining towns and camps. They had no limited fields and worked wherever they wished or wherever they decided to stop.

The oil shares were the most attractive to the miners. There was so much talk about riches in oil. The agents had obtained through a scheme the addresses of the miners. They were put on a mailing list, then circulars began to roll in day by day to the miners. The circulars described that oil was being struck and thousands of barrels were being produced daily. They showed the figures that profits were rolling in to the investors that were fortunate enough to buy some of these shares in these rich oil wells.

At the bottom of these circulars, printed in large colorful letters was an invitation that there were a few chances for men to be lucky enough to obtain the first 1000 stockholders group. After using the circulars as forerunners, the agents followed up and then the harvest began. However, when the agents found that in some camps the situation did not go as they expected due to the stubbornness of some miners, they used a famous and special strategy to draw the miners into their net.

At some of the camps where the miners did not fall for the bait, they would go into the camp and find a few scattered families that they could sell a few shares, and when that was a success, the agents knew the camp was theirs for the taking.

After they had succeeded with sales of the stocks, the agents would keep away from the camps for about sixty days. Then they would return again with great news that those who bought the stocks made great money. The news was extremely alluring.

Yes, they brought dividends for a few lucky investors that had bought the oil stocks just sixty days ago. Of course, even the investors were surprised, and quite sorry that they did not buy any stocks at the time when they had the opportunity to buy. They thought that a lifetime opportunity was knocking on their door. They were sorry because a lucky star was smiling on them and they ignored it. What's more, the dividends were larger than the actual investments in the original oil stocks.

Of course, the proud investors of such holdings in oil and gas stocks began to buzz and brag over the entire camp on how their good investment brought them over 100 percent dividends, clear profit, in a short sixty days.

Well, this famous strategy did it. Everyone at the camp heard the good news about the oil investments and large dividends. After that had happened, every miner in the camp, including the women were eager and ever willing to invest as much as they possibly could.

The agents were remarkably busy for the next few days at the camp. The miners waited impatiently on their front porches with money in hand. They waited for the agents so they would not miss out on such a swell and particularly good profitable investment.

Thousands of miners at that time owned the best security that money could buy. The American United States Liberty Bonds with a very reasonable margin of interest.

The miners began to exchange the bonds at a sixty percent rate for the gilt-edged worthless oil shares. Many of the agents had spread rumors that the bonds would become valueless shares in later years and they would be difficult to get rid of them. Many miners accepted the rumors as true as the rumor spread like a disease all over the mining region. Eighty percent of the miners fell for the rumors and were trying to get rid of the world's best security for a worthless piece of paper.

Fifty dollars on a hundred-dollar bond was the highest price the agents would accept. The agents were pretending that the bonds are not likely desirable in the deal, however, if there was no immediate cash, they accepted the bonds. But most of the time their offer was forty percent on the dollar.

After the agents had cleared the gates at the camps, their mission was complete. They disappeared forever. Many of the miners still holding their gilded edged certificates and shares as a memory. And from time to time, they would dig them out from the bottom of their trunks and glance at them with a heavy sigh and saddened thought. The artistry of the gilded edges of the shares and certificates with various colors and designs still fascinates them deeply. Now it is only a sad memory for thousands of the coal miners.

Occasionally they warn their children or grandchildren not to fall as they did for a get-rich-quick investment as they pulled their shares from the trunk to show them as proof as what they had just spoken.

Now let us turn another angle of the investing field. Let us find out where the miners who did not invest their money in the oil and gas scheme.

During and after the First World War, and during these most prosperous years, the automobile industry expanded to be the greatest manufacturer of many different types of automobiles.

Money was plentiful, and the manufactures of the automobiles begin to get new ideas. More newer models were being created and turned out. And the more models they made; they realized the more money they could make. They also found out that the common classes of people liked the different models put out on the market. As soon as a new model would appear in the show rooms, the people immediately would exchange their old car for the new model. All it took was about four or five hundred dollars and a small monthly payment. Under these conditions there were no difficulties for the miner to buy a new car every year or sometimes more often.

Yes, those were the good years of prosperity. Plenty of work, plenty of money. Everyone had money. While the masses were making money, they were willing to spend freely and carelessly. During those prosperous years, a small percentage of miners remembered and saved for the rainy days. Many of the miners refused to believe that the most prosperous era will someday come to a sudden end.

Some have saved and bought homes or farms and held onto their good and best security, Liberty Bonds. But most were caught unprepared, surprised with large debt, and left penniless at the end of those great, prosperous years. Years that would never be witnessed again for many years.

While some of the masses of working people were emerged in the prosperity, enjoying and sharing the good times, a disastrous end was nearing and millions of people were not prepared for the abrupt end of prosperity.

# XX

## MIRACLES HAPPEN

A few weeks later, Father Daniel and Gip had a heartfelt talk. When Gip had admitted of the theft and ransacking of the club's goods, Father met Gip on the street. Father Daniel asked Gip to drop into his office as soon as possible, saying he had something especially important to discuss with him. For some reason Gip Erceg became alarmed. He feared that Father Daniel would make him pay for the goods he had stolen and damaged or report him to the police if he refused to pay. Gip shivered from all the thoughts that came into his mind. Gip thought that Father Daniel must had talked with Rev. Karin and Dr. Graymore and they decided to insist Gip pay for the goods or have him arrested.

But how can Father Daniel do such a thing? He is a priest. He had promised him that nobody would ever know of the theft, only the two of them. No, he cannot, his promise bound him to silence. Yes, he promised that he would never reveal the robbery as long as he behaved himself and stay away from being the leader of the gang. Gip gathered up enough courage and decided to meet with Father Daniel regardless of whatever it may be. Indeed, that was Gip's blessed decision that would change his course of life entirely.

"Come in, come in, Gip." Father Daniel greeted Gip as he knocked on the door. "Come in and sit down, Gip. I want to talk to you about something that may interest you," remarked Father Daniel.

"Hope it's something good," said Gip as he settled into the chair that Father Daniel offered him.

"Gip, would you like to go along with me on a short trip? I have got some business to attend here and there, so I will be away from home and be on the road for a few days. I will be more than glad to take you with me. What do you say, Gip? Do you want to come?"

"Oh Father, you don't want to take me with you. You know I ain't no good. Everybody looks at me as an outcast. I cannot understand it, Father." Gip uttered these words with some bit of sadness. Then he spoke again. "Then I would have to ask my parents for permission whether I can go, and probably they would never consent that I can go because I was always very bad."

"You do not have to get consent from your parents, Gip. I already asked them and they heartily approved that you may go with me if you wish."

"Oh gee, Father, I would love to go. I never was away from this camp in my whole life, but I may be a burden to you on this trip," Gip quickly responded with sparkles in his eyes.

"Alright, Gip. Be here tomorrow after Mass, about ten o'clock or sooner if you can. You need to take nothing with you. Just put your best dress suit on and be here in the morning."

Joseph Gip Erceg, for the first time in his life, thought that Father Daniel is the best person in the whole wide world. However, Gip still had a burden, a secret deep down in his heart. This disturbed him lately very much. But he thought, maybe on this trip he would forget it.

The following day, Father Daniel and Gip Erceg drove away from the camp in a one-horse buggy borrowed from Dr. Graymore. Gip did not realize that Rev. Karin and Dr. Graymore knew the secret and the mission of Father Daniel's trip with Gip Erceg.

On their way, Father Daniel and Gip visited several towns, including Pittsburgh, where Father Daniel was also a caller at the bishop's residence for purely diocese business.

After several days, Father Daniel's business was transacted and they were on their way home. Perhaps it was Father Daniel's plan that they have been caught by the darkness of the night in the neighborhood of the reformatory school. Father Daniel then suggested that they spend the night at the institution, and after a good night's rest, they would resume their trip home.

Father Daniel spent twenty-four hours at the institution with Gip, just to get him interested in the routine and drastic system of the lads who were mischievous as Gip. Gip did see with his own eyes the treatment the lads were receiving for their past behavior, maybe their behavior was less bad than his own. Thoughts began racing in his mind. Gip's thinking accelerated and started guessing whether Father Daniel brought him there and he will reveal his robbery to the warden of the institution. *What should I do?* To escape now, to escape immediately before Father Daniel gave him up.

Seeing the reform school must have had a great bearing on Gip's morale. He had seen things that he would not want to happen to him. His inner self must have stormed between evil and good constantly. Gip had regretted every moment of his awful days of the past. He wished now that his conscience were clear and peaceful and if he could only pay for all the damage that he had committed against others.

Gip remained silent on their way home. Never speaking one word for a long time. Father Daniel also remained silent for quite a while. He knew that Gip needed time to meditate, time to decide whether to remain on the road to crime and human ruin and destruction or turn to the road that would give him a happy life and a decent world and society.

As they traveled and got closer to home, Father Daniel knew Gip was struggling in his interior. He left Gip to decide for himself once and forever, what road he would choose for his future life after he had witnessed good and bad.

When Father Daniel deemed that the storm had passed in Gip's mind, he broke up the long silence and spoke to Gip. "Well, Gip, how did you like the trip? Did you see or hear anything that was of interest to you? Have you learned anything? Or did you not enjoy the trip?"

Father Daniel paused and gazed ahead toward the animal that had been pulling the vehicle in which they had been riding. He was concerned whether Gip was going to answer his questions or not. However, it appeared that Gip was kind of glad, somewhat happier that Father Daniel had broken the long silence. Gip's face seems brightened as he formed a faint smile as he glanced at Father Daniel and spoke.

"You bet, Father, I learned a lot on my first adventure, on my first trip. Really, I enjoyed it very much. I do not think that I can ever find enough words to thank you, Father, for what you did for me." Gip suddenly paused, and he had become frightened about something, but this only just lasted a moment. He again raised his head up and spoke. "You know, Father, when we left home for this trip, I came with you having horrible thoughts in my mind. After you had invited me on this trip, I made up my mind from the very beginning to rob you and run away to some big city and join one of the big gangs."

Before Gip could say another word Father Daniel suddenly interrupted him and said, "Gip, we are still far away from home. You still can rob me, or even kill me. I still got some money left that will take you to a big city. However, this money does not belong to me, I borrowed the money from Dr. Graymore so we could have enough for our trip." Father Daniel paused and glanced over at Gip, who was silently listening to Father Daniel's soft words that were spoken and cut deeply into his heart. Then he again spoke. "What difference it is to be a gangster. All he wants is money and even if he had to kill to get the money, it would not matter. You still want to rob me, Gip?"

Gip's eyes were filled with tears. With grief and sorrow, Gip slowly said, "I don't want to rob anymore. I have seen enough on this trip; there is an op-portunity for every lad in this country who wants to try for it. I also have seen the rewards for crime." Again, Gip paused. His interior was fighting for some decision, he was afraid or hesitating to reveal something that lay on his con-science. Again, he spoke. "I have seen in the reformatory what a boy's penalty is for bad and evil behavior. I have learned a lot, which changed my mind on the way I shall want to live. Yes, Father, if it was not for you, I might be on my way to big crime, and perhaps the electric chair."

"I am glad, Gip, that you have seen the difference in life," Father Daniel remarked with a smile on his lips. Gip's face brightened and suddenly became gay and happy. Now he had made his decision that just a few moments ago, appeared disturbed.

Gip put his arm on Father Daniel's shoulder and said, "I've got a confession to make. Remember the first week after you came to the camp? Do you remember the church collection that was stolen from your satchel? Well, I stole the money." Gip paused and grinned at Father Daniel. "It was $190. After I got the money. I got scared and did not know what to do with the money. I hid the money as soon as I got home. I will bring it to you. I have been afraid that I would get caught sooner or later." Gip sighed with great relief. A true confession for the first time in his life. This relieved him that had been laying on his mind ever since he stole the money. Gip was now free of nightmares, which had been pursuing him ever since he had the money in his possession.

As they neared the home, Father Daniel had fallen into a deep and heavy thought. His youthful life came back to him. His colleagues and their families. Now he is glad and happy that he is what he is.

He now did not envy his colleagues any longer who were in higher position, or may have successful businesses, who may be famous lawyers and doctors, who may have wives and families, who may have wealth and more freedom and enjoyment in life. He stopped caring for all the worldly luxuries.

Indeed, Father Daniel was glad and happy that he was sitting near Gip in the moment. The boy that in the very beginning of his life, could have been destroyed and separated from principles of humanity and society.

Isn't it worth sacrifices to save others from human destruction? Yes! At that moment Father Daniel was the most content person in the whole world. A joyful and happy expression had appeared on his long-worried countenance as he spoke again. "Gip, next year you will be finishing your grade school. Wouldn't you be interested in a higher education? As for instance, a priesthood? Or maybe a doctor or a lawyer? Do you have any plans, some ambition for your future life?"

Gip stared at Father Daniel with surprise in his eyes. In his past, Gip never gave thought to such a thing like education. His only ambition was to be a gang leader. He never thought of his future life until he saw the reformatory institution.

His past was full of bad behavior, and he never gave any thought about his future. But since Father Daniel had mentioned the future, he finally realized that he must forget about his past forever, and seek a new field of adventure, an entirely different adventure from his past.

"Father Daniel, you know it's impossible for me to think of a better education than you just mentioned. You know my father is a coal miner. He hardly makes enough to provide for our family for the necessities of life. Eventually, I'll follow my father's footsteps to be a coal miner, a human worm." Gip spoke these few last words with some disgust.

"Gip, I'm sincere and serious with you. I know what I was saying and want you to get what you have missed. Do not misunderstand me, Gip. There is always a way if one has ambition." Father Daniel further suggested, "You see Gip, many young boys like you win a scholarship every year to some higher educational institute, college or higher places."

Father Daniel related to Gip, step by step how to achieve something if he tried with all his effort. "They earn their scholarship for something that they have achieved in their lower classes. You, and any other boy in America have the same equal opportunity, to receive the same education as the next one did."

"Yes, yes, but what have I achieved? My record of mischief and many pranks are written in every classroom in the county. Yes, Father Daniel, they would never give a scholarship to a boy with my record. No, Father, I think it is useless to talk about it," Gip said, bowing his head low with sorrow in his eyes.

The trip with Father Daniel opened Gip's eyes and gave him a lifetime lecture. But what can he do about it now? His school records would never give him another chance. They will not trust him anymore, even if he tried with earnest.

Gip remained silent, and nothing interested him in a better education. Father Daniel presumably knew Gip's thoughts. He left Gip alone in his thoughts for a while. He knew that Gip now would give his right arm if the records of his behavior had been erased from the schoolrooms, and other public places.

Father Daniel again interrupted the silence. He took Gip's hand in his, and gravely said, "Gip, I am going to make a promise to you, or rather a far-reaching proposition, and it will depend on you to change your future life and become a worthy citizen of this wonderful country." Father Daniel paused again and gazed steadily into Gip's eyes.

But before Father Daniel could speak again, Gip interrupted, saying, "Father Daniel, no matter what you promise regarding the proposition you made to me, I already resolved that, from now on, Gip is going to be another different Gip Erceg, you wait and see." Gip made this declaration with a glorious expression in his eyes. And Father Daniel saw another Gip Erceg.

"Gip, honestly I promise you that if you conduct yourself properly in the classroom during the coming year and I receive a satisfactorily report from the principal, I will get a place for you in one of the colleges, or perhaps the place where I commenced my studies."

"Father Daniel, you are a real chap. You are the truest companion that a boy could ever have. I will promise you, Father, that from now on, you will not be disappointed in me. So, help me God."

By that time, Father Daniel and Gip reached the end of their long journey. They finally reached the camp, and Gip bid a good-night to Father Daniel and rushed to his home with thoughts dancing in his mind.

Gip became a different lad entirely. He began to read good books and the Bible daily. Gip very seldom went out on the street with other boys. Gip wanted to stand by his solemn promise that he will begin a new life, that he will try his best to erase his bad records from the schoolrooms and try to convince the teachers that he had given up his mischievous pranks, and Father Daniel will never be disappointed in him.

Father Daniel watched every move and deed of Gip. He became very satisfied with Gip's conduct since the journey. He began planning for Gip's future and was ready to make any sacrifices that may be required. To bring Gip back and retain him with God's grace.

Gip was a frequent visitor at Father Daniel's parish home. Many times, Gip consulted Father Daniel for advice in his studies and also his religion. Gip needed that advise to maintain his proper conduct.

In his early years, Gip never paid much attention to school and religion. After Father Daniel arrived at the mining camp, Gip was as far away from religious thought, that it would be impossible to bring him back into the fold. In his school, he never was interested in any subject, except recess and

Saturdays, Sundays, and holidays. He did learn how to read and write, that is all he cared for in class.

Now Gip regretted for all that he missed in the past years, and that is the reason that he visited Father Daniel so often. To seek advice and information. And in the coming school year he would gain as much learning as he could, to make good the promise he had vowed.

# XXI

## THE HARVEST

A year has passed, and the three modern Magi were certain that they had conquered the evil among the youngsters at the camp. The sport activities became immensely popular among the younger generation and were supported generously by the entire community. Yes, the grownups as well as the older folk loved to see their children engaged in sport activities. The three men added to the sport two more loops in each church, which they called the junior loop and senior loop. The sport calendar was active all year round. After the baseball season ended, they organized football teams, and through the winter months, they organized basketball teams, which were a great success.

The pranks and mischief hat had developed to an uncontrollable situation at the time when Father Daniel and Rev. Karin arrived at the camp. At the present, the troubles had fallen to a minimum, which was the greatest satisfaction. To the three great brave men who gave all the effort to succeed in the endeavor of ridding the mining camp of troubled youth.

A few years have passed and everything was very harmonious at the mining camp. Dr. Graymore since we last heard of him got married. He was the happiest man with his wife and two children. Rev Karin, after several years of struggles at the mining camp, finally got used to the common mining people.

He finally loved the whole community and decided to settle in with the people in the mining field. He also got married and had a small family of his own.

What a contrast, Rev. Karin, Dr. Graymore, both have families and were very content. At the end of a long day's work, both have a home of their own, both have someone waiting for them in the evening when they return from their daily tasks, their wives and children.

And Father Daniel, at this particular time was quite content and with a very satisfied life. He is happy and content because the members of his congregation are happy and content. The whole congregation are always in a harmonious way and give Father Daniel total cooperation.

He was content with the children in his parish that being taught Christianity, that the word of God was rooting in their tender heart and that peace and happiness had smiled on the camp.

Father Daniel sighed with relief, as he sat in his office and reviewed at a glance, the work he has done since he arrived at the mining camp. He was happy with what work he had accomplished in his chosen field since he arrived at the camp. The much-forgotten wildness of the youngsters in this difficult mission was a total success. He sighed with satisfaction and felt somewhat proud of his past years. He feels somewhat at ease that the burden he had carried for years has greatly lessened. Now he can take life easier after the hard and strenuous work for many past years. Yes, he earnestly was entitled. He rightfully earned to take life easier after years of hard work.

As he sat at his little desk as thoughts roamed about the past, his eyes gazed down over his desk, and a large envelope that he must have misplaced in the morning mail lay there waiting to be opened. On the upper corner of the envelope indicated that a decision had arrived from the bishop's chancellery. He was not in a hurry to open the envelope, but instead let his thoughts roam in the past. He stared at the letter for a while, for he thought that was the only letter he had regularly received each week. Sometimes two letters arrived from the bishop in a week. As he continued to stare at the letter, with laziness, he opened the envelope and stared at the written letter for a while. His hands were shaking helplessly on the desk. Large tears appeared in his eyes and slowly rolled down his cheeks and dripped on the open letter that lay on the desk before him.

The letter was official from the bishop. It was brief, but it stunned Father Daniel. It was the bishop's order informing Father Daniel that he was being transferred to another location, which will be effective in thirty days.

A new field with new surroundings, new people, new children. Everything new again. Possibly worse and harder than the mining camp he was about to leave. Will he have the same hard work as this mining camp that he just brought into full harvest? Will he have or meet another Gip Erceg? Will he have the same evils facing him daily?

He knew that the bishop's orders were final and nobody can ever change his orders. Father Daniel dropped his head into his arms as they lay on the desk and cried silently like a child. Finally, he fell into a long sleep. It was late into the night when he woke up. To strengthen his stormy interior, he spent the rest of the night in silent prayer.

The following Sunday, Father Daniel announced his departure by reading the letter from the bishop to the congregation. He read the letter with great emotion, which brought many parishioners to tears. Many that were present in the church just would not believe that Father Daniel would have to leave them.

The members of Father Daniel's church had their thoughts in the air. They did not want to hear that Father Daniel was about to leave them. They called a meeting at once and decided to send a committee to the bishop to retain Father Daniel. Even people from Rev. Karin's church attended the meeting and heartily sympathized with the congregation. For the good Father was everybody's friend at the camp, the whole community.

Yes, Father Daniel was loved by all, young and old, even the colored peoples came to Father Daniel many times for advice, whether it was just common words or something spiritual. They all had confidence in Father Daniel.

Father Daniel realized that the parishioners felt grief and sadness. He shared the grief with them. But there was no alternative in the bishop's order. The bishop's order was final! He knew that it was useless to create further difficulties regarding this matter.

The following Sunday, Father Daniel advised his congregation to be patient and abide and obey the bishop's order. He assured them that the bishop will send them another priest in his place before he leaves. He further advised them that the bishop knew best where the spiritual needs are needed. The congregation heeded Father Daniel's advice and submitted to the bishop's order. Nevertheless, the entire community was in grief over Father Daniel's departure.

Many children that had been reared under Father Daniel's guidance loved him dearly. The youngsters who played many years of sports under Father Daniel's eagle eyes will lose their leader, their most loved advisor and their real spirit. They will miss him. He will never be forgotten.

The congregation now realized that Father Daniel will soon leave, and they will not let him depart from them until they show him some token of appreciation and love.

The men and women of the whole camp got busy and went to work. They have planned a farewell party with an appropriate gift for Father Daniel remembrance from the whole community.

Then people from the mining camp were very generous. Catholics, non-Catholics, negroes, the entire community wanted to be present at the farewell party of Father Daniel. Yes, everyone wanted to shake his hand for the last time. Everyone wanted to hear Father Daniels last farewell words to the thousands he knew, and that knew him.

Just two more weeks before Father Daniels departure. As usual, he sat in his office at the little desk working on reports and books so that the new pastor will find everything in order when he arrives.

As Father Daniel sat at his desk, there was a slight knock on the door. Father Daniel arose to greet the person on the other side of the door. He hesitated for a moment thinking that this may be the new priest who will replace him at the little church. A thousand thoughts were going through his mind. What shall I say to this new priest? I hope he will be as happy and content as I was in this mining camp. Will the community like him? What will he be like? Who was he?

Father Daniel opened the door slightly and very slowly. Fear struck him momentarily. He finally opened the door and to his surprise and total shock, it was Gip! Gip Erceg, now Rev. Erceg. Tears filled his eyes and a smile broke out on his face as wide as the Monongahela River. They both reached out at each other at the same time and put their arms around each other with a hug that seemed like it would never end. Father Daniel's mind was racing with a thousand thoughts. This little mischief gangster has completed the seminary and is now a priest. What a miracle! Nobody in the mining camp, the entire community would believe their eyes when they will be introduced to their new priest.

*Oh, how the good Lord works in strange ways*, thought Father Daniel. At this moment in time, Father Daniel was the happiest human being in the world. Words could not describe Father Daniel's feelings.

As the two sat down to talk, old times began to rattle in both priests' heads. They began to speak about the times they spent together, both good and bad. But many times, they found themselves speechless because of the shock Father Daniel was carrying in his interior, in his heart, and in his soul.

Gip, now Rev. Erceg had kept the promise he made to Father Daniel years ago, that he would stay away from evil and do the best he could. He would study hard and become a good societal member. Rev. Erceg made it from mischief and gangsterism to be a man of God, the teacher of the Bible. Nobody will believe this when Rev. Erceg will be introduced to the congregation.

Sunday approached quickly. The entire community became the congregation of the little church. They all wanted to meet the new priest. How would they react from what they will see?

Father Daniel and Rev. Erceg slowly walked into the little church, the entire community turned toward the opening door and looked up. Shock could be felt in the entire state of Pennsylvania upon staring at their new priest. There were so many mixed emotions. Tears in some eyes, gasping in others. "This is a miracle!" someone shouted. Some got down on their knees and thanked God for what they were witnessing. A local coal mining man of mischief and crime has become a priest. A man of God!

Father Daniel opened up his sermon with a joyous and most happy announcement introducing Gip, Rev. Erceg. The community knew him from the past, but were so excited about what they were seeing, all their past thoughts fled from their minds. Yes, every soul was happy in this particular camp, the entire mining community.

Yes, they were extremely happy for two reasons. First, because for the very first time, a young man from the mining camp had achieved and succeeded to priesthood from the rank of a foreign coal miner. Second, because of the fact that a young boy who began his life with mischievous and pranks that led to gangsterism and became a menace to the mining camp, made a total turn around in his life.

The congregation again began planning. A twofold party was in the making. A farewell and welcome party was in progress in the little mining camp. The women of the camp began to gather up like busy bees to make the party a success.

During the week, Rev. Erceg permanently arrived home, to the camp. A group of home folks waited for him at the parish yard to welcome home their first priest from their camp.

Rev. Erceg stayed at Father Daniel's house most of the time where Father Daniel was giving him final instructions and preparation to administer to the church congregation.

Fatherly and softly, Father Daniel prepared Rev. Erceg on his hard future road of his new life. Father Daniel softly said, "Father Erceg, remember that in your future life, you will be loved, hated, and persecuted many times during your life as a priest."

Finally, the long-awaited Sunday has arrived. The crowds began to gather around the church early in the morning. Long before the ceremony had started. The little church was too little to house everyone that arrived from the community. Catholics, non-Catholics, Protestants, Lutherans, Methodists, Baptists, atheists, negroes, the entire community was there to see the first boy from the camp ushered into priesthood, a teacher of the Gospel.

For the occasion, Father Daniel prepared a very impressive sermon, a sermon of Rev. Erceg's life. He began his sermon with the very first day he arrived at the camp. Then he narrated step by step how young Erceg began his mischievous life from his childhood. He told the crowded church how Rev. Erceg committed many thefts and caused damages and how he enticed others.

"No," Father Daniel explained, "to advance so far from building up a gang of other boys in the camp and starting to menace the entire community to make it to priesthood is a miracle that we are witnessing before our own eyes." Father Daniel, after narrating Rev. Erceg's life, said. "With God's will, Rev. Erceg came from being a thief, a gang leader, a bandit, a criminal, an outcast of human society from which he designed for his future life and this miracle happened. God has changed his will and sent a call upon him to become a priest, to sow the word of God, to be a preacher of the Gospel."

Father Daniel paused long enough to wipe heavy perspiration from his brow. He gazed over the crowded church where he saw tears glisten in many eyes. Then he added, "Only God knows. Someday Rev. Erceg may be your spiritual counselor, your priest, your pastor. That he, who once menaced your camp and your community, someday he may become your friend. Yes, he could be compared to the prodigal son. He, too, failed, but God's call was not in vain. If it will be God's will that he was sent here, accept him as your own. God bless you."

The party was of rejoicing and grief. The rejoicing was of Rev. Erceg's achievement to priesthood, but the grief was the parting with Father Daniel. The party was proof of hard work of the three men, Father Daniel, Rev. Karin, and Dr. Graymore.

Father Daniel has parted from the camp with consolation and contentment. His heart felt easiness and his mind was peaceful. He sensed to himself that the sacrifices at the camp were worthwhile. Behind him at the camp, he leaves an incredibly happy congregation and a young priest. This was his reward for his hard and strenuous work. But there was something else that Father Daniel carried from the mining camp.

When Father Daniel arrived at the camp several years ago, his black bushy hair which showed a few gray hairs here and there, changed to gray, and only here and there you could spot a black hair.

It was his memories from the mining camp. He saw a lot and he learned a lot. He saw hundreds of misfortunes among the miners and their families. He saw hundreds of family's dreams and plans destroyed and opportunities snapped from out under them.

His heart grew with theirs and he loved them dearly. He felt with them every hardship, every misfortune and every catastrophe. His sympathy was always with them. He was a consolation to every mining family.

Rev. Karin and Dr. Graymore lost a very dear friend in Father Daniel, for he was the spark of their little organization.

Tears appeared in Rev. Karin's eyes as he shook Father Daniel's hand and whispered, Goodbye."

Dr. Graymore's ever-smiling mood also disappeared as he parted with his good old friend.

Indeed, many thousands, young and old, Catholic and non-Catholic alike grieved after his departure. Yes, Father Daniel was remembered for many years after he left the camp.

# XXII

## LIFE AT THE CAMP

Life at the mining camp is very colorful. In every house lives a different nationality. One could hear many different languages spoken on the mining villages streets. The migrant population grew rapidly in the early 1900s.

Every other house was filled with boarders. Some were coming and some were leaving. The camp street always remained crowded with different nationalities. In those years work was plentiful in the mining area that men changed different camps quite often. And a steady stream of foreigners was arriving from the Palace in New York by train constantly and moving into different camps.

One could see men coming and going to and from work every hour of the day and night. The coke yards began to work at midnight, you could see the coke workers emerge from dark alleys of the camp with pitchforks on their shoulders marching toward the coke yard.

The coke ovens near to the camps, were like a flaming chain that spurted its flames toward the sky, which gave ample light several hundred feet around the plant and camps.

In about a half hour after the coke yard workers began to work, one could see large clouds of white steam ascending into the sky from watering of the burning coke. In about four in the morning, miners began gathering around the mine to receive their orders and enter the mine to work. The miners who were working the night shift were returning home.

As the coke workers who were returning from work in the coke yards, another shift of miners is gathering for their afternoon shift. Late in the night a final crew of men enter the mine. And this repeats itself over and over, day, afternoon, and night shifts are entering the mine as the previous shift is leaving. This is the miner's life at the mining camps.

Early in the morning, wagons loaded with kegs of beer make two to three deliveries a day. Each brewery has its own agents, and every agent has their own wagon. There were also whisky agents making deliveries twice a week. It was quite common for whisky agents to deliver two-hundred gallons of whisky to the camp in one week.

Wherever there were ten or twelve boarders in one house, the beer cellar was never empty. There were always several kegs of beer in the cellar.

When the miners returned home from work, they usually washed in the kitchen in a large tub. The boarding mistress's duties was to wash every boarders back and after the washing was done, which took two hours or more, supper was served. The supper mostly consisted of soup and homemade noodles and a meat which was boiled in the soup. It was cut into pieces on a large square board and set on the table with a jar of mustard. This was the miners main meal, day in and day out.

After the supper was served, a keg of beer was tapped, and the boarders would sit around the table and play cards while the beer was passed around. During many such evenings, two or three kegs of beer were easily consumed before the men retired to bed. In those days, a four-gallon keg of beer cost seventy-five cents and a gallon of whisky cost from a dollar fifty to three dollars depending on the quality of the whisky.

In the good old days as they were referred to during this coal mining boom, living was unbelievably cheap, and even cheaper when more boarders were located in one house. The boarding mistress bought the groceries and meat on her own name in the store, and at the end of two weeks or payday, the entire bill was divided equally on each man. Each share amounted to four to five dollars per man, including beer and whisky.

In some houses, the boarders were good to the mistress, they were good sports. The boarding mistress was not excluded from her share. She was getting three dollars a month from each man for her work, which included bed, washing, cooking, laundry, and all other services that was needed to maintain the workers. However, where the boarders were misers and greedy, they insisted that the boarding mistress must pay her share as any man in the house. Whenever there were children up to fourteen years of age, they must pay half share for each child.

Peddlers with trinkets and notions, took advantage with their harvest among the foreign population, especially the boarders. The foreign miners never saw such things as safety pins, hair ornaments, broches, beads and a vast diverse varieties of trinkets. Especially those that came from rural countries in Europe. The boarders bought these different kinds of trinkets as valuables and stocked them in their trunks to take them home with them when they would or if they returned to their native lands.

Many times, the peddlers sold out their goods in one house when the boarders were all at home. Fancy towels, mantel pieces, handkerchiefs, top shirts, underwear, ties, socks, thimbles, cheap penknives, and many other notions were sold out in a short time. Like hot cakes.

Whenever the boarders ran out of money, the boarding mistress had to reach for her pocketbook and pay for the goods the boarders had bought, and then collected money due her on the coming pay day. However, some of the peddlers left the camp with sad memories of dealing with the miners, a new experience they kept in their mind for future dealings with the foreign miners.

I remembered what happened very clearly not long after I arrived to one of the mining camps. One day a peddler knocked on the door. It was Saturday, just after sunset. The house consisted of twelve boarders. The peddler was welcomed into the house. As usual, the peddler spread his bundle in the kitchen on the middle of the floor. He opened his satchel and unfolded everything he had on the kitchen floor. The boarding mistress also sat down on the floor, and the boarders surrounded the peddler. They circled around him. Everyone was anxious to see what the peddler had in his satchel and bundles. The articles were passed around from hand to hand, and the peddler could not keep his eyes on everyone. He kept his eyes on the goods which were on the floor and in his satchel. He had a smile on his lips that his goods were going rapidly and he was doing a very satisfactorily business.

The peddler saw his entire bundle and satchel were empty, but to his surprise, only a few men held an article or two in their hands which they said they had bought. Where were the rest of the goods? The men who held the articles they had bought paid for their goods. But who was going to pay for the rest of the goods that disappeared between the men's hands.

The peddler could not prove that anyone stole the items and did not see anyone walk out of the house. He was so busy with his bundle on the floor, that he could not understand how the goods disappeared.

However, this was planned long before the peddler came to camp and knocked on the door. The men handled the goods from hand to hand and then towards the second-floor stairway where one of the boarders was hidden who just put his hand out when the goods were passed as he piled them up on the stairway and then carried the goods to the second floor.

Of course, the peddler did not raise much questioning, fearing that he may get beaten besides the loss of his goods if he demanded payment for the goods. He left the house with empty hands, that an hour ago he entered with fifty dollars of articles.

This was his new dear experience. But he decided then that he would never knock and enter a house of boarders the rest of his life. However, other peddlers would go through the same experience as he did. They would learn the same way. For this is the life in a mining camp.

Holidays, weddings, and christenings were crucial days for the mine officials. On those occasions, the mine and coke yard suffered greatly. Many times, the mine and coke yard had to shut down entirely for a few days until the events had passed, which some of the time had to shut down the whole week.

Many of the foreign men thought that they were musically inclined. And many of them bought a musical instrument. They bought accordions, violins, bull fiddles, flutes and clarinets. On Saturday and Sunday nights, one could hear an echo of music over the entire camp. Singing, whistling, the playing of many different musical instruments. There was singing and music in many different languages echoing all over the mining camp.

This was the life in the mining camp. Youngsters playing on the ash-covered streets. Some playing baseball on the other end of the street. Farther up, the youngsters were playing marbles for keeps. And at the opposite corner, they were playing "carry corner."

A baseball crashes through the window, a carry fell into someone's garden, another lad hit someone with a bean shooter. On an open porch a young man was courting his sweetheart. That is the life in a mining camp in the beginning years of the coal mining industry.

Yes, my dear reader, in those days there were no beer gardens, there were no automobiles, there were no moving pictures, no radio, not even a phonograph.

At nine in the evening, young and old were all inside of the house to retire for the day, to refresh for the coming morning.

Yes, this was the life of the mining camp when coal mining was in its prime. When the coal mining camps were born in the hilly counties of southwestern Pennsylvania.

# XXIII

## THE GREENFIELDS

Harry Greenfield, whose parents immigrated from England some fifty years ago was a well-known man all over the region. He was well-liked around the mining field.

Harry piloted many mines in the early 1900s over the mining region as a mine foreman and was a very experienced and practical mining man. He was well-liked because he was a fair and impartial foreman to the average working miner.

The Greenfields were well-off and a good standing family. They have three sons and two daughters: Harry Jr., eighteen, Wanda, sixteen; James, thirteen; Hubert, ten; and Vilma.

Harry Jr. just finished his high school with very satisfactory and remarkable marks. He finished high school with high honors. His parents considered very seriously to further his studies in college. Wanda was in her second year of high school. James just finished grade school and was preparing to enter high school in the coming fall.

The Greenfields dreamed and wished to see Harry Jr. become successful lawyer, or some high-up executive. Wanda also had her dreams. Many times, she expressed to her mother that she wished to become a high school or college teacher.

Of course, every parent wished to see their children obtain the best education that they could afford. Like the Greenfields, they, too, wished that their children would be inspired ambitions and wishes fulfilled and achieved if they felt that they could afford to further their children's education.

The Greenfields even with a sizable family were able to save several thousand dollars for the purpose of a schooling fund, to give their children their desired education.

However, it was not enough to put their children through school as the desired, but they hoped and counted that those at home would work and contribute to help the older children get their education. And as one completed their education, they would help the others through their education.

Those were the dreams, the plans, and wishes of the Greenfields. Harry Greenfield while relaxing during the evening hours had constantly dreamed about his children's future. He had pictured his children starting with Harry Jr. to become a highly successful attorney. Yes, an exceedingly popular young lawyer. He envisioned Wanda as a great teacher at one of the high schools or colleges. James, Hubert and Vilma were also pictured in Harry's mind. James could be a doctor with the financial help of Harry Jr. after he got settled.

Hubert could be a minister. And Vilma, well, there is plenty of time to plan for her future. *Let us get the oldest through first and then we can plan for Vilma's future. The rest of the children will take care of her*, pondered Harry Greenfield.

In the autumn of 1920, Harry Greenfield Jr. entered one of the foremost colleges in the state. In the same year, Wanda had taken a summer course in one of the state teacher's colleges to help her when she would enter college.

Harry's first year of college showed to be very promising. His study in college was highly satisfactory. The college teachers praised his effort of his first year.

But the Greenfields gasped when they felt the first burden of the college expenses. They began realizing that college was awfully expensive and costly. However, they were ready to make extreme sacrifices for their children betterment of their future life.

In the late spring the following year, Harry Jr. came home on a short vacation for a period of two months. This was his second year in college. Harry was looking forward to his studies. He kept dreaming far ahead on becoming a lawyer.

Wanda was preparing to go to the teacher's college the following fall. She had finished high school also with high honors as Harry Jr. did.

After the first world war, work around the mine was plentiful and wages were very reasonable compared with other industries. The entire mining region prospered. But like anything else, things get out of order caused by a few people that spoil good things.

It was early in the spring when strange faces appeared around the mining camp and on the streets where men gather, and finally, they showed up at the mines. Later on, it was found out that the strangers had come to the mine as agitators, as labor organizers who wished to establish a labor organization in the mining field. Just at the beginning of the summer, the agitators had succeeded and pulled the men out of the mine and commenced with a strike against the mine officials. The men responded at a hundred percent. Many of them were glad to just get a good rest. Thousands of men quit their jobs and left the pits without knowing why they were quitting.

The first few months were smooth and quiet. The men spent their time in preparing gardens, playing cards, attending mass meetings, sometimes twice a day. The men just loved the strike that was called. They did not worry much because every family had some money saved.

Harry Jr., being home on vacation wished he could make some money during his free time to help his school fund. He wanted to make a few dollars for spending money at the college. But he hesitated to go to work in a time like this when the men were striking.

Finally, upon insistence from the plant superintendent, and his father, Harry Jr. went to work, not in the pit, but on the outside yard. This work did not interfere with the striking men. Nevertheless, some of the strikers got irritated and began to make threats to the Greenfields. Despite the warnings from the striking workers, the students could not be barred from any work if they chose to work as long as it did not interfere with the strike.

The strikers were determined to stay out of the mine until the operators of the mines yielded to their demands. But the operators of the mine decided to fight the strike to the bitter end, until the miners willingly returned to the pits.

The companies then began to import men from other fields, known by the strikers as strike breakers. Late in July, the strike breakers began to arrive by the hundreds to the mining pits while the strikers had to stay out. This further irritated the strikers because they saw others taking their jobs. Some of the striking men began to lose faith in their leaders.

The strike situation had stiffened. It was heard here and there that clashes between the strikers and strike breakers had occurred at many of the mines. The strikers wanted to stop the importation of men to work in the pits, but these men resisted. Many a mornings resulted in fistfights between the two groups of men.

At one particular plant where the Greenfields had lived, a clash had occurred between a striking miners and the men that were working in the mine. It was just a few days before Harry Jr. was to leave his job because of the threats. Harry Jr. had planned that he would take a few weeks rest before returning to college. But his plan resulted in tragedy.

The clash had developed into gun violence. Several shots were fired, but nobody knew who fired the shots. The striking men claimed that no striker had carried a gun.

The clash repeated again the following morning. A stray bullet hit Harry Jr. and penetrated his abdomen, but he miraculously escaped death. Through a skillful operation of a specialist, Harry's life was saved. However, the doctors feared that Harry Jr. will be partly disabled for the rest of his life.

Harry Greenfield Jr. spent two- and one-half years in a hospital bed until he finally recuperated. Harry returned home, partly disabled and with a blank future. Even if he wanted to finish his studies, this would be entirely impossible. The Greenfields had spent every cent they saved to save Harry's life. Besides their own savings being wiped out, they had to borrow money to pay their other bills.

State and county authorities investigated the shooting and made several arrests. But after questioning the suspects, they had to release these men on account of lack of evidence. Until this day, nobody knows who fired the shots that destroyed Harry Greenfield Jr.'s dreams and ambitions.

Harry Greenfield Sr. squarely blamed the shooting on the mine plant officials, claiming that the strike breakers provoked the shooting. All his loyalty and faith were lost toward the company. Two weeks later, Harry Greenfield was dismissed as mine foreman at the plant. Harry Greenfield, once well-known and a well-liked mine foreman became a common jobless man as thousands of others. Harry Greenfield joined the ranks of the striking miners.

This incident prevented Wanda from entering college as she had planned, wished, and dreamed about for years. All the plans of the Greenfields had to be postponed until a future date. Until when? How far? How long? One year? Maybe two? Who knows? No one knows.

Approach of the first snow was at the threshold. Rumors were spread that here and there men were returning to work in the mines. The rumors were partly true. The men began to get restless. Little by little the men deserted the picket lines. Some went to other fields to seek employment to avoid humiliation.

The mine owners took a drastic action. They decided and petitioned the court for eviction of the striking miners from their homes which was property of the mining companies. A wholesale eviction began in the mining camps. A ten-day notice was served on the miners to either return to work or vacate the homes in which they lived.

The evicted mining families were unloaded at the edge of a public road with their belongings and left there to their own fate.

To quiet dissatisfaction and embarrassment of thousands of families, the union leaders speedily had to build barracks to shelter the families before the heavy snows would begin. A hard winter would trap the families on the road to nowhere.

New and strange people began to move into the dwellings once occupied by the striking miners. Many of the older miners saw this situation develop and many began to fear that they would be pulled out of their many years of employment.

Finally, news was dispatched that the strike had been called off by the union. Many of the miners felt humiliated and never returned to the same mine but changed to other mines or looked into other fields of work. However, the majority of the miners were forced to remain where they previously worked because of their financial hardship.

Those remaining in the mining region scrambled for some kind of work in the mines. But many of them were greatly disappointed. A few months later after the strike was called off, the mines began to slacken and there was no work, mainly, for the striking miners.

It took many years for many of the striking families to get back on their feet. The greater part of them were caught in the circumstances of the Depression. No money, no work, and most of all, no decent home to live in.

The Greenfields were no exception. With uncertainty of the future, the once immensely popular and well-off Greenfields, with beautiful dreams, plans, and wishes just a few short years ago, stared into the darkness of the unexpected, dreadful incoming depression.

Under these circumstances, the Greenfields had abandoned their dreams, their plans to educate their children.

Wanda accepted cheap clerical work near her home to help the family pull out of the rut into which they were dragged by strange circumstances, not by their will. The rest of the Greenfields remained near home seeking some kind of employment to restore the family to get back on their feet.

Wanda's dreams and ambition to become a college teacher never came true. Through worries and hard work, and anxious to see her family build back as when she began her sweet and happy dreams, Wanda contracted complications of sickness and after five lingering years, she died of a broken heart.

Yes, Wanda Greenfield paid the ultimate price. She paid the supreme price for others' mistakes and errors. In the prime of her life when she began think of a beautiful future, just like a bud of a sweet flower, her life was snipped off merciless. Just because of evil humanity.

During these years, Harry Greenfield Sr. advanced in his age and was never able to take a responsible job as he once held. He found work in the mine as an assistant foreman, but that did not last. He was being attacked by rheumatic pain, which interrupted his work occasionally.

Harry Greenfield Jr. obtained clerical work at one of the local mine offices and tried to support the still hoping family.

Thus, another family with beautiful dreams, with plans and hopes, with ambitious children, remained just a memory.

Perhaps another generation of Greenfields may restore the dreams, hopes, and plans that the Greenfields had hoped for years. But for the time being, the Greenfields remained just as many thousands of miner families, just dust eaters, human worms.

# XXIV

## THE DEPRESSION

Late in the summer, just at the beginning of fall in the year of 1927, a slight slackening of coal production was felt in the coal mining industry. The smaller operators began to operate their mines only three or four days a week. The larger operators still worked a full schedule but hiring of new men ceased entirely. It was impossible to obtain a job at any of the mines that were still operating full schedule. Many miners opined at the time that the mine slackening would pick back up in a few weeks. But the operators taking inventory, repairing furnaces at the steel mills and factories began to lay off men.

But thousands of miners presumed that after a few more weeks the mines would be operating with full force, But the miner's opinion was greatly wrong. Before the winter set in, the larger operators began to slacken their mines and began closing some of the mines permanently. Thousands of men were dismissed and those that obtained employment had to travel at least sixty miles a day to work.

Then came the fatal year of 1929, the crash of the stock exchange. With the crash, it seemed the whole world slumped with it. Factories, mills, mines, and other industries began closing down. Millions of men and women were thrown out of work all over the country. In the years of 1930 and 1931, very few mines worked. And those that did work, were working only two or three days a week. Business enterprises began closing their doors. Bankruptcy of smaller businesses at the beginning of the Depression were a common occurrence everywhere.

Just before the Depression hit the country, many thousands of the miners had purchased new cars with high monthly payments that had to be met regularly. The miners also had other large purchases and monthly installments due to the goods being bought on credit. The collectors began threatening to seize their properties, if payments were not made in a certain time specified by the creditors. Some of the miners considered themselves fortunate because they had a few dollars deposited in the banks that they depended on to make their monthly installment payments.

What a disappointment. The banks one by one began closing their doors, and before the average miner could withdraw their money from the bank, the bank was either shut down or stern restrictions were put on withdrawal of money. Yes, a disappointment was felt not just among individuals, but equally among businesses, organizations, schools, churches, societies, lodges, hospitals, and many other industries throughout the United States. Many of these business never recovered.

As previously mentioned, many thousands of miners just before the stock exchange crash occurred, contracted themselves with high-priced automobiles and other household luxuries that required high monthly installments. This was entirely impossible for the miners to meet their obligations when the Depression arrived. Many of the miners found themselves in despair and ruination.

Chaos, panic, and fear prevailed throughout the mining camps. Hunger and poverty sets in the mining camps and immediate aid was needed for many mining families because they were on the verge of starvation.

Upon action of many civic organizations, churches, and other humanitarian societies appealed and voiced for immediate action to prevent hunger and illness among the thousands of children and women. The plea was heard and action was taken. Federal, state, and county authorities sought some kind of relief for millions of hungry and unclothed citizens.

Yes, the Depression came suddenly, unexpected for millions and millions of unprepared people. Finally, relief agencies were set up in every community.

However, these were new and inexperienced agencies. There was experimenting with an allotting system for relief in many communities and the administration for relief alone consumed half of the relief money that was allotted to the community.

At the beginning of the relief allotment, which was the most necessary for the home, was given immediately to the starving families. Warehouses and wholesale establishments were rounded up for any excess foods and immediately given to needy homes. Foods that had been sitting in warehouses for years were hauled away to the relief centers for distribution to the needy.

It was a pitiful scene. Men and women standing in extremely lengthy lines with bags and sacks in their hands waiting for their allotment of food. From early in the morning into late in the night the lines were steady. Many people that were towards the end of the line were disappointed because the food had been totally dispersed.

Some cursing, some mumbling, some with tears in their eyes turned back to their homes with empty bags, with worry and grief written on their faces, with hunger on their lips. "What are my children going to eat tonight? What shall I do?" Mothers whispered to themselves.

Those were the crucial days for the miners, especially for wives and mothers. The flour bin empty, the cupboard looked like a farm after an auction sale, empty. Grief and worry made many mothers hair gray during the Depression. Many mothers lie in their precious graves because of suicide and broken hearts because they had no way to feed their families.

In those days, in those dark days of the Depression, the miners ceased to dream and plan of their future. The dreams and plans, the wishes and ambitions of their children that they carried so dearly in their hearts existed no longer. All their plans and dreams had been set back, postponed, but more likely destroyed forever. Many became tired and disgusted with life and did not care what would happen to them.

The coal miner lived in constant fear, fear of the future. The was no certainty, no assurances for tomorrow's meal. This was the life in those days of the never-forgettable depression of the years of 1929 to1932. The Depression was merciless to all, whether they had their money in bank savings, investments, or in other places, they were affected equally. All were stripped to the bone of everything they possessed without exception.

These were the living memories of the coal miner and their families during the darkest days of the Depression. Financially indebted, physically ruined, and morally defeated by worries and hardships.

Millions lost their savings, their hard-earned money, their homes, land, stocks, shares through educated speculators. They lost everything because they were unable to meet their contracted obligations.

As a result, many became drunkards, beggars, and family evaders. These men could never come back to a normal way of living. When the Depression lessened, thousands of older miners could not obtain jobs due to their advanced age. There were no means of supporting themselves so they had to rely on relief from charitable organizations until the day they departed this earth.

Thus, the Depression destroyed thousands of the miner's dreams and plans for their talented children's ambitions for the future. He was indebted so deeply that it would take him years before he could breathe more freely, more securely without fear to the future.

Now at this point in the mining camp, his sons were ready and willing to help, to begin their own life's dreams and ambitions. But there was no immediate work for them. For the miner fortunate himself that he was employed.

The miner waited patiently for the time that work would resume all over the country. That his sons could obtain work so he could help pay off his long-overdue obligations.

The Depression was slowly vanishing, but the miner did not dream as he did a few years back of his children's education, of their talent, but his only dream was that his son would find employment.

In due time, his dreams will come true. His sons may get employment and they would be able to help him and then begin lives of their own. They will get married and their lives will begin anew, yes anew.

This was the miner's new dream, new wish, to get his family on their feet again, to give them a new start in their young beginning. The miner began to smile once in a while as his worries lessened day by day. His sons and daughters gained employment one by one. He began to conquer his fear of uncertainty.

He began to think that the future would be brighter and prosperous and that happiness again will prevail in his home.

But alas! As his young son, who obtained employment just a few years ago and could now buy himself a good suit of clothes, was preparing a good life for a family, World War II struck in Europe. He had to forget all about the coal mine where he began his future living, he had to leave and learn another job. To shoot, to kill, and to defend his country.

That is the life of a coal miner. He dreams, he plans, he wishes as he constantly thinks how to achieve his plans and dreams. But this sudden war has destroyed all his plans, all his dreams and plans for the future This mere human worm must now become a warrior with absolutely no certainty that he will ever return to his adopted land, the United States of America.

# XXV

## FILBERT! WHERE OUR LIFE BEGAN

Grandpap settled early in the twentieth century in the mining camp called Filbert. His family settled in a company house, the same company house where I grew up in the 1950s and 1960s. There were three rows of these camp houses and we lived in the third row that was situated near the top of the hill, house number 85. The houses were two floors totaling four rooms where my parents squeezed seven of us into the four rooms: a living room, a kitchen, and five children in one bedroom in two small beds.

The house was heated by a small coal stove that sat in the kitchen. The stove never adequately heated the house. In fact, we always huddled in the kitchen around the coal stove called a *heatrola* to stay warm. A small, rounded edge refrigerator stood in a kitchen corner that had to be defrosted every day. There was no indoor bathroom during my younger days. We had to go thirty feet up the hill to the shanty (outdoor toilet, outhouse) when nature called. This was absolutely no fun during the winter months. We washed in a concrete sink located in a six-by-six-foot pantry and mom washed clothes in that sink with a scrub board. But to the mining families, this was normal everyday living, and nobody ever complained. This was the life of a coal mining family.

The road that ran between the second and third row was a mixture of gravel and tar that remained bubbling hot throughout the summer and continuously slippery during the winter months constantly covered with coal ashes. There was no such thing as a streetlight.

My dad was a man with a black face, a human worm, a coal miner. When he worked, he would arrive home blackened from head to toe covered with suet and coal dust. There was little change over time in the coal patch. We had friends with nick names such as Mutzie, Gibby, Piggy, Buckwheat, Huba, Poogie, Rabbit, and Moon. Well, they called me Naked Al, but that is another story.

Daddy would work two or three days a week. Times were tough. There were no food stamps, and not to be hungry, the entire family, no matter how young, had to go to the little red brick schoolhouse with sacks in hand and were issued World War II surplus food. A container of canned beef, powered eggs, cheese, a pound of lard, a bag of sugar and flour and a few other items. Our income was less than a thousand a year for seven of us.

There were a number of small coal mining patches similar to Filbert called Buffington, Fairbank, Orient, Searights, Herbert, and Footdale, all located in a four-mile radius. Youngsters were all the same throughout the patches. We played in the coke ovens during the day, barefoot most of the time. And as we grew into our teens, most of my friends became coal miners except me, I joined the US Army and ended up in Vietnam.

On December 6, 1962, my dad went to work on the midnight shift at Robena Coal Mining Company, Frosty Run Shaft. He was on the shift to go down into the pit next. However, there was a huge explosion at the Frosty Run Shaft leaving thirty-seven men mutilated and dead. Since my dad was on the next shift to go into the pits, he ended up being a rescue worker. Down in the pit, a mine cave beam collapsed and hit him on the back of his head. Less than a year and a half later, my father was dead at forty-one years of age. This mine accident still weighs deeply on the families of this mining disaster sixty-one years later. The lives of coal mining families never change.

Let us take a short walk to the end of Filbert patch and meet the Umbel brothers, Alan, Kenny, and Bo, all former coal miners. We will get acquainted with the Umbel's and get educated with today's mining family customs and habits, worries and fears.

Between the three brothers, they have eighty-seven years of mining experience in the pit. Nowadays, there are a few women working in the mines. In fact, Alan Umbel's wife was one of the first women to go down into the mining pit. At present, the only functioning mine in the region is Cumberland Mining company.

The boys went on describing life under the earth. Dark and very cold in the winter and wet and cold in the summer. The dust problem no longer exists in the pit. The United Mine Workers of America protect the miner from dangerous situations such as dust and gas. Each miner wears a dust monitor, and if the monitor collects too much dust, the miner does not have to ride the elevator into the mining pit. They also wear gas monitors, nicknamed "canary," to measure the methane gas that has accumulated in the mine. They went on telling me that the nickname came because they used to send canaries into the pit before the miners descended into the mine. If the canary did not come out, it died because of too much gas. Today, all miners must wear a battery operated digital monitor attached to them at all times wherever they go in the pit. Also, they wear a tracking device so they can be located at all times and easily found if there is a cave-in or another dangerous situation occurs. But overall, the mine is extremely safe just from thirty years earlier.

The Umbels all responded in unison about today's miner. The young miner tends to be non-union because they are paid a few dollars more. However, they must go into more dangerous situations if the bosses tell them to. They said that the vast majority of mining accidents happen in non-union mines. What it comes down to with the non-union miner, **"it is all about the money."** They all emphasized that the UMWA pushed hard to protect the miner. They are proud to have great pensions and health care coverage in their golden years.

Life at home is no longer a struggle for the family. The women no longer has to slave for hours keeping the family above the poverty line. Their children go on to college, the women hold their own career, and life is normal as any other middle-class family.

The Umbels wanted to end the conversation on the mining in the pit and wanted to discuss the "war on coal." They became quite angry about the climate change/global warming alarmist. They expanded the conversation by calling this movement a bogus religion. They would never be submissive to a false religion and bend a knee or bow down to the climate change/global warming religion. "They are at war with us and we are only simple people," one of the brothers states. "It will collapse like all false religions do." Another stated, "It is the largest financial and economical hoax ever thrust on the American people. Why do they so badly want the elimination of fossil fuels? It is all about control of the people."

Kenny Umbel talked about most miners being fisherman and hunters. He states, "We take good care of the planet. We always pick up litter before we leave. We make sure that all sparks from our fires are put under. We never trash our waters and land. We support natural gas, oil, nuclear energy, and **clean coal**. We are not against electric and solar energy. To depend just on electric and solar energy cannot happen when over 35% of electricity comes from burning of coal." They all complained how China continues to use fossil fuels without word from the climate change alarmists.

The conversation was finally over. I got in my car and drove off, constantly thinking what I was told by the Umbels. After a few moments I had a quiet conversation with myself and came to a final conclusion. "It is always dark and cold being 700 feet under the earth. You are alone at times and on constant mental guard. Probably thinking about their wishes, dreams, hopes, and ambitions. What a difficult job to have in your life. These miners will always remain dust eaters, underground farmers, mere human worms, and men with black faces."

## THE END

www.ingramcontent.com/pod-product-compliance
Lightning Source LLC
Chambersburg PA
CBHW070801160726
48004CB00001B/274